MANNERS *of the* HEART
Lower Elementary School Curriculum

Kindergarten
By
Jill Rigby Garner

Contributing Author, Shawna Gose, MS

MANNERS *of the*
HEART®

Baton Rouge, LA

Published by MANNERS of the **HEART**®
215 Royal Street
Baton Rouge, Louisiana 70802
225.383.3235
www.mannersoftheheart.org

Curriculum Specialist: Candy Jones, M.Ed.
Graphic Design: Ashley Daigle
Cover Design: Brian Rivet
Merryville Stories: Nick and Jill Garner

Table of Contents

Table of Contents

Acknowledgements

CONTRIBUTORS
Thank you to those who contributed to the creation of this curriculum, our local teachers, staff, consultants and friends:

Polly Allen
Katie Barker
Debbie Charbonnet
Leah Goodman
Melissa Hamel
Candy Jones, M.Ed.
Kate Kleinpeter
Laura Lombardo
Samantha McCartney
Shawn Mills
Jeani Moniotte
Jessica Neel

Mary Frances Neuner
Chelsey Newnham
Rachel Palmer
Shirley Papillion
Danna Sabolik
Sara Snyder
Carter Stone
The Arc Baton Rouge
The Dunham School
Ffion Thomas
Lexi Verret
Jennifer Young

Lori M. Smith, M.Ed., Editor
Raymie Bell, National Board Certified, Copy Editor

SPONSORS
Thank you to the foundations who sponsored the creation and piloting of this curriculum:

The Boo Grigsby Foundation
The Huey and Angelina Wilson Foundation
Blue Cross and Blue Shield of Louisiana Foundation
Albemarle Foundation
The Powell Group Fund

PILOT SCHOOLS
Thank you to the schools who piloted this curriculum:

Children's Charter School
LaSalle Elementary School
LaBelle Aire Elementary School
Our Lady of Mercy Catholic School
The Dunham School

Introduction

Can you imagine how different our classrooms would be if every child had self-respect and showed respect for others?

Wouldn't you enjoy a school environment filled with young people who were more concerned with what they could do for others rather than what others could do for them?

Manners know no social or cultural boundaries. Common courtesy and respect for others should be part of everyday living no matter where you live. Customs may differ from one region to another, from one side of town to another or from one country to another, but treating others with respect is a universal need. Defining manners as an attitude of the heart that is self-giving not self-serving, Manners of the Heart® teaches children to respect others, and in the process, they gain respect for themselves.

Manners of the Heart was founded to help you help your students become respectful youngsters who grow up to become respectable adults. After more than ten years of working in schools, from the inner city to the suburbs, from the rural South to the affluent West Coast, we have identified the real problem that has plagued our educational system.

In the early '70s, specialists began telling us the secret to raising successful children was to build their self-esteem. Books on the subject skyrocketed to the top of best-seller lists, encouraging us to be friends with children, not authority figures. Discipline was out, praise was in. We stopped encouraging children to persevere until they achieved greatness. Instead, we told them they were the best just for *being*. Thus, the "sticker revolution" began, the idea that children deserve rewards for everything.

Here we are forty years later faced with plummeting test scores, escalating violence among even our youngest students, paralyzing entitlement and the highest drop-out rates in the history of our educational system. The evidence is clear—self-esteem is not the cure, but rather the culprit.

Manners of the Heart® has the solution. Heart education must be the foundation for education.

At Manners of the Heart®, we don't tell children they're great; we help them become great. We don't tell children they're the best; we help them become their best. We don't teach children to do the right thing for a reward, but rather to do the right thing because it's the right thing to do. The outcome—their self-esteem is replaced with self-respect and self-control.

Schools experience a rise in academic scores, a decrease in disciplinary actions and an increase in parental involvement. Parents are equipped with tools for effective discipline, motivation and the ability to raise respectful children in our disrespectful world. Students develop respect for others and self-respect, enabling them to become all they are meant to be.

Manners of the Heart® is here to stand with you in educating your students for life and living.

| **7**

How to Use this Curriculum

Manners of the Heart is here to help you help your students. We are an evidence-based character education program designed to strengthen morals, improve social and emotional skills, and increase respectfulness. This curriculum has been carefully studied, researched and tested in the lives of children.

Manners of the Heart will help you:
- Increase prosocial behavior in your students
- Develop a sense of personal responsibility and work ethic in your students
- Replace entitlement in your students with the motivation to achieve a goal
- Empower your students to self-regulate their behavior
- Boost empathy in your students

The results in your classroom and in your students:
- Reduction in bullying incidents
- Reduction in time spent managing disciplinary actions
- Decreased conduct problems, hyperactivity, and emotional symptoms
- Increased teacher effectiveness
- Improved academic performance

INCLUDED IN THE CURRICULUM KIT:

- *Manners of the Heart* teaching manual
- **My Manners** Intranet access
- Wise Ol' Wilbur the owl and Peter and Penelope raccoon puppets
- 25 *Manners of the Heart* folders for home/school communication
- Monogrammed *Manners of the Heart* teaching apron

ORGANIZATION OF MANUAL

Twenty-two lesson plans are divided into four parts: **Attitudes of the Heart, Everyday Courtesies, Communication Skills** and **Living in Community**.

Each part is divided into weekly lessons, which include the core teaching (approximately 20 minutes) and four or more **Extended Learning** activities (5-15 minutes, depending on the activity chosen) for daily reinforcement of the core principle.

The introductions and **Big Ideas** for each week's lesson offer the central theme for all grade levels, enabling the instructor to know the objective being taught at each age—especially important in first through third grades for the review of lessons from previous years.

The weekly lessons are organized as follows:

Attributes—Two or three traits the lesson instills in the heart of a child. (Definitions of traits

How to Use this Curriculum

found within the text and in **Wilbur's Glossary** in the Appendix.)

Skills and Objectives—Grade specific ideas the lesson teaches.

Materials and Preparation—A list of supplies or preparation needed and additional activity sheets or stories found in the manual.

Wilbur's Words of Wisdom—A phrase, poem, cheer or thought that offers the main teaching point.

Guiding Children's Learning—Instructions to follow in teaching the core lesson.

Extending Children's Learning—Four or more additional activities to use each day of the week to support the core lesson. These activities integrate other academic subjects and skills.

Home Connection—A letter to send home to parents or guardians to keep them informed and engaged by offering further training for the child in the principles of the week's lesson.

THE APPENDIX

Common Core State Standards Chart—Academic standards addressed in *Manners of the Heart* lessons. To learn more about Common Core, visit http://www.corestandards.org/.
Pre and Post Assessment Instrument—A tool to evaluate student prosocial behavior.
Activities and Attributes Chart—A glance at the instructional methods used to teach lessons.
Materials Chart—Supplies needed for each lesson.
Extended Learning Academic Alignment—Breakdown of applicable subjects and skills included in each activity.
Wilbur's Glossary—Clear definitions of attributes.

INSTRUCTIONAL SUGGESTIONS

We recommend instituting **Manners on Monday** with the teaching of the core lesson, followed by the **Extending Children's Learning** activities Tuesday through Friday. Reinforcement of the core lesson is a critical component in the success of the program as repetition instills the qualities presented in each lesson in the hearts of your students. To support your inclusion of *Manners of the Heart* throughout the week, our **Extending Children's Learning** activities incorporate our concepts into other academic subjects. You can also integrate **Wilbur's Words of Wisdom** throughout the week by writing them on a board in your classroom or having children recite them each morning.

NOTE for kindergarten and first-grade teachers:
It is recommended you learn each Merryville story to be more engaging in telling (instead of reading) the story to these younger audiences. This will also provide you with the opportunity to shorten the story, if necessary, for younger grades who have a limited attention span.

How to Use this Curriculum

HOME CONNECTION

Monday is also a good day to send the **Home Connection** letter to parents or guardians to encourage reinforcement of *Manners of the Heart* lessons in the home.

DISCUSSION QUESTIONS

Within **Guiding Children's Learning**, discussion questions are provided for you to ask students in the teaching of the lesson. After encouraging the children to give their own answers, our *Manners of the Heart* answers are provided in italics following each question. These are included as the critical points children should receive for full instruction.

MASTERFUL STORYTELLING

Several lessons include *Manners of the Heart* stories set in the fictitious town of Merryville. These stories are filled with comical characters and creative story lines that illustrate the principles being taught. The stories engage the imaginations of students, opening their hearts to internalize the principles being communicated. In preparing for the lessons that include a "Merryville" story, you and your students will greatly benefit from animated storytelling. Below are helpful hints to becoming a master storyteller:

- Read the story several times to become familiar with the setting and the characters. Read it aloud to hear the cadence of the words and to experience the story as the children will experience it. Do your best to familiarize yourself with the story enough that you use the story as a guide, rather than a story you must read.

- Use your own imagination to 'see' the town of Merryville and the characters. Close your eyes and smell the salt water as you walk along the beach with Tommy in "Tommy's Treasure." Visualize the leaves of the happle tree rustling when Wise Ol' Wilbur peers out to greet folks passing by. The more you 'see' Merryville, the more the children will 'see.'

- The main characters are Tommy, a ten-year-old boy with a good heart; Wise Ol' Wilbur, the crusty owl with great wisdom and Mrs. McDonald, the widow of Farmer McDonald, who knows the history of Merryville and bakes the best cookies in town.

- Practice using different voices for the main characters. Wilbur's voice could be somewhat high-pitched with a bit of a grumble. Mrs. McDonald's voice could be that of a sweet grandma. Tommy's voice is that of a young, inquisitive boy. By changing voices, you present not only the story line, but also bring life to the characters' personalities.

- Stand in front of a mirror and pretend you're sharing the story with your class. Your facial expressions should change according to the intensity of the story line. For instance, when Bully steals the ball from PD in "A Bully's New Heart," your face should show Tommy's displeasure with a look of disgust (scrunched mouth and brow) as you're telling the children that Tommy followed after Bully to recover the ball. In other words, your face should show the words you're saying.

How to Use this Curriculum

- Use exaggerated animation. If the character in the story moves, you should move. When Tommy finds himself lying on the ground underneath the happle tree after losing control of his bike, you should look up, too. When Carolina the Cow whispers a bit of gossip to Helen the Horse in "Who Said You Said," you should lean in to whisper, too.

- Play the roles of the characters as though you are performing in a play. Be sure to speak clearly with a crisp tone of enthusiasm, whether that means with sadness, happiness or anger. You'll feel silly at first, but you must exaggerate the emotions to make them real. Raising the pitch in your voice to show emotion can be irritating to the ear of the listener. Instead, intensify your expression.

- The great advantage you have over radio is that you have all the qualities of communication at your disposal. Not only do you have words, pitch and tone of voice, but most importantly you have body language. Use each to the fullest, especially eye contact. When setting the stage for the stories, make eye contact with your students. Help them to join you in Merryville by inviting them in with your eyes.

- If you really want to master the art of storytelling, record yourself and listen. You'll be amazed at how much you can improve by listening to your own voice.

- Storytelling is bringing the words on the page into the hearts of your students, so they can 'see' the story through the eyes of their hearts—their imaginations.

- Put your heart into it! Your students will love you for it. The added benefit is the enthusiasm they show for your storytelling may just spill over into enthusiasm for your teaching! Creative storytelling opens a child's mind to possibilities beyond their circumstances through their imaginations. When their imaginations are ignited, the possibilities of what they can do and who they can become are endless, creating a passion for life and learning.

- Encourage your students to put their hearts into the stories they read. Offer opportunities for your students to become masterful storytellers. Bring new meaning to "Show and Tell" with the idea of 'showing' the story as it is being read.

Remember, Merryville stories are meant to teach, not just entertain. Your masterful storytelling will engage students in the initial lesson, but you can continue referring to the Merryville characters throughout the week to remind students of any lessons learned. For example, "What do you think Wilbur would say is the right thing to do?" or "Do you remember how good Tommy's heart felt when he gave away his treasure?"

How to Use this Curriculum

YOUR HAPPLE TREE

You can add Wilbur's "Happle Tree" (explained in "Welcome to Merryville") to your classroom by using an artificial or bare-branched tree in a corner of your room. Students can help cut out a bushel-full of construction paper happles (hearts with two leaves) to hang on the tree each week during the *Manners of the Heart* lesson time. **Wilbur's Words of Wisdom** from each lesson can be written on the happles before hanging to remind students of the lessons learned.

THE PUPPETS

Young children are fascinated by puppets. They are willing to set aside reality and accept what a puppet has to say. If you are willing to act a little silly, we recommend use of the puppets as much as possible—especially in moments of stress. If a child displays unwanted aggression, puppets are a great way to diffuse the situation. Wise Ol' Wilbur, Peter, and Penelope puppets are available through the Manners of the Heart® online store at www.mannersoftheheart.org/store/.

TECHNOLOGY

The *Manners of the Heart Elementary Curriculum* is technology integrated, enabling 21st century learning. Your children will enjoy seeing the Merryville graphics on your interactive whiteboard as the enrichment lessons are taught, or even during math class for a fun word problem. Integrating these graphics into other subject areas is a great way to remind children of their *Manners of the Heart* lessons.

The Intranet portion of the Manners of the Heart® website is located at www.mannersoftheheart.org under the **My Manners** tab, which includes:

- Lesson introductions, lesson plans, activity sheets, Home Connection letters
- Interactive whiteboard flipcharts (utilize with any ActivBoard, SMART Board, etc.)
- Weekly morning announcements
- Merryville graphics (png files of characters, town scenes, and map)

Intranet access is included in the purchase price of a curriculum kit. If your school purchased the kit, contact your school administrator to obtain your login information. If your kit was an individual purchase, contact Manners of the Heart® for your login. If a manual alone was purchased, an Intranet access subscription is available for an additional fee. Contact Manners of the Heart® at info@mannersoftheheart.org.

COMMUNITY SUPPORT

Manners of the Heart offers your school an excellent opportunity to utilize community partnerships. Many businesses in your area are concerned with the quality of education for the next generation and are willing to help. The lessons of *Manners of the Heart* can be effectively taught through volunteers teaching the core lesson and teachers reinforcing core objectives through **Extending Children's Learning** activities throughout the week.

How to Use this Curriculum

FREQUENTLY ASKED QUESTIONS

Q: Who should teach the lessons?

A: *Manners of the Heart* is a flexible curriculum that can be taught by classroom teachers, counselors, or volunteers. Regardless of who is selected to teach the weekly lessons, here are some key points for classroom teachers to keep in mind:

- **You will produce the best results when** *Manners of the Heart* **is consistently taught and reinforced over the school year.** We recommend scheduling your core lessons to be taught on the same day at the same time by the same person, with one lesson per week.

- **You will produce the best results when you set a time for the program.** Work with your administration to create time for *Manners of the Heart*. Integrating *Manners of the Heart* into a core academic curriculum works best, such as social studies.

- **You will produce the best results when you are engaged in the weekly lessons—even if you are not the one preparing or teaching the core lessons.** If you are not teaching the main lesson, make sure to still remain in the classroom to participate in the content with students. You will need to be keenly aware of the content that students are learning in order to reinforce key objectives throughout the week, thus sustaining a general culture of respectfulness within your classroom.

- **You will produce the best results when lessons are taught to students in your/their own classroom.** Location is important because students are more often reminded of the prosocial attitudes and behaviors when *Manners of the Heart* is taught in the same environment where they are learning throughout the day.

- **You will produce the best results when you consistently model respectful behavior for your students.** Children respect those who respect them. They are also far more likely to internalize what they *see* rather than what they *hear*. At Manners of the Heart®, we ask teachers to sign a pledge that they will practice the same respectful behavior students are learning through the curriculum. None of us can be perfect, but we can do our best to be a good example for our students. We can humbly respond with an apology when we mess up and lose our cool.

- **You will produce the best results when you make time to read each lesson introduction.** The introductions are meant to inspire the person preparing to teach the lesson. Rather than giving detailed instructions, they are

How to Use this Curriculum

- filled with illustrations of the principles being taught to aid in the presentation.

Q: When should lessons be taught?

A: We recommend instituting "**Manners on Monday**" with the teaching of the core lesson, followed by the **Extending Children's Learning** lessons Tuesday through Friday. Each week will then kick off with a new idea on manners and respectfulness that can become your classroom's initiative for the week.

Q: How should lessons be reinforced?

A: Reinforcement of the core lesson is a critical component in the success of *Manners of the Heart* as repetition instills the qualities presented in each lesson in the hearts of your students. Each lesson includes four or more **Extending Children's Learning** activities for homeroom teachers to reinforce the core lesson. For the most transformative change in your school, we recommend doing as many of these extended learning activities as possible. These activities make it easy to incorporate *Manners of the Heart* concepts into other subject areas (see charts in the Appendix). Students will also complete a variety of crafts or activity sheets throughout the curriculum, and we encourage educators to hang these in a prominent place in their classroom or hallways for the rest of the week as a reminder to students. You can also integrate **Wilbur's Words of Wisdom** throughout the week by writing them on a central board in your school, reciting them with students through your morning announcements, or writing them on a board in your classroom.

The Intranet portion of the Manners of the Heart® website (located at www.mannersoftheheart.org, **My Manners** tab) includes additional resources to enhance lessons. For example, **Morning Announcements** offer an additional opportunity to reinforce the core teaching of the weekly lessons. Many schools include these in internal memos and/or in newsletters for community-wide distribution. Interactive flipcharts can be used in a computer center for students to review *Manners of the Heart* lessons and concepts. Merryville character graphics can be utilized for story starters, math word problems, etc.

Q: Can I involve parents?

A: Each curriculum lesson includes a **Home Connection** letter for parents or guardians, educating them on the content their child is learning and offering practical suggestions for reinforcement at home. Monday is also a good day to send the **Home Connection** letter home through the student folders that are included in each kit. Student folders can also be used to send home progress reports! If you did not purchase a kit, a bundle of 25 student folders is available through the Manners of the Heart® online store at www.mannersoftheheart.org/store/.

How to Use this Curriculum

Q: Can I involve my community?

A: Manners of the Heart® offers your school an excellent opportunity to utilize community partnerships, as curriculum lessons can be effectively taught through volunteers teaching the core lesson. Teachers can then reinforce the core lesson with the **Extending Children's Learning** activities throughout the week.

Q: What about table manners?

A: In addition to the 22 lessons on character, Manners of the Heart® offers a social skills curriculum on table manners called *Manners of the Heart At the Table*. Table manners lessons can be implemented in much the same way as your character lessons; each lesson, however, is divided into a 10-15 minute lesson for the classroom and a 5-10 minute lesson or reinforcement for the cafeteria. Our recommendation is to make the 22 character lessons your main priority during the school year. However, if cafeteria courtesy is a concern in your school, as it is in most, we recommend implementing *Manners of the Heart At the Table* at the end of the year following your conclusion of character lessons. Table manners lessons will provide great reinforcement of the general attitudes of courtesy and kindness that students learn through the character curriculum. The *Manners of the Heart At the Table* manual includes 10 lessons on table manners appropriate for elementary students in grades K-5. The manual is available through the Manners of the Heart® online store at www.mannersoftheheart.org/store/.

Q: How can I assess the program's impact in my school?

A: The *Manners of the Heart* manuals include a pre- and post-survey for teachers to complete before and after program implementation. This 37-item assessment instrument measures changes in students' hearts based on their actions and attitudes. Teachers should compare the results at the end of the year to determine changes in class behavior. As a suggestion, this survey can easily be adapted to measure individual student prosocial behavioral changes. The assessment is located in the Appendix.

If the Manners of the Heart® program has been implemented school-wide, you should also look at some of the cultural trends in your school. A great measure to assess changes in school culture is the *Respect & Responsibility School Culture Survey* (2012). Best given annually, this 29-question survey developed by the Center for the 4th and 5th Rs assesses the extent to which everyone at school acts with respect and responsibility toward others. This free instrument is available at http://www2.cortland.edu/centers/character/assessment-instruments.dot. Please note that such cultural shifts often take longer to notice than do changes in individual student prosocial behavior.

Manners in Merryville

It has been said that educating the mind without educating the heart is no education at all. Manners of the Heart® couldn't agree more.

If the heart needs of a child are not met, a brilliant mind will be wasted. The education of the heart *should* be the heart of education.

During our "Listen to the Children" study, Manners of the Heart® interviewed more than 400 children, ages five to fourteen, from all walks of life. We quizzed the children with questions ranging from "Do you do chores at home?" to "What's a family?" Their answers were enlightening and, at times, downright convicting.

The question, "What's more important, being smart or being nice?" is a prime example of the insightfulness of children:

- "I want to be nice because that will make me smart."
- "If you're not nice then you're not smart."
- "I must be smart cause I try to be nice."
- "Nice." (96% of the children responded "nice" without hesitation)

The children knew the best answer. They knew that head knowledge and heart knowledge are intertwined: one cannot be separated from the other. When we attempt to educate the mind without educating the heart, "We create a menace to society," as Theodore Roosevelt once said. At Manners of the Heart®; we believe the quality of the heart determines the thoughts of the mind, as well as the resulting words and actions.

Just imagine what our world could be if the next generation is equipped with not only head knowledge to lead, but also heart knowledge to lead in the right direction!

16 |

Introductory Lesson: Manners in Merryville

Our vision is to provide professional heart education programs designed to strengthen morals, improve social and emotional skills and increase respectfulness, thereby developing character in the next generation.

The core values taught through *Manners of the Heart* are the following:

- Manners are an attitude of the heart that is self-giving not self-serving.
- Manners are not a set of rules to be followed, but rather principles that guide behavior.
- Manners are based on respect for others and self-respect.
- Self-respect *must* replace self-esteem.
- It is more important what we give the world than what the world gives us.
- To open the mind, you must first unlock the heart.
- It's more important to *be* good than to *do* good.

It is our duty to educate the minds of students. It is an honor to educate their hearts.

Sir Walter Scott said it well: "We shall never learn to feel and respect our real calling and destiny, unless we have taught ourselves to consider the education of the heart."

In this week's lesson, children will be introduced to the meaning of manners through *Welcome to Merryville*. The story is not just intended to instill manners in the hearts of your students, but to engage their imaginations as they are introduced to the Merryville characters. Encourage your students to join other children who have enjoyed Merryville with the 'eyes of their hearts.'

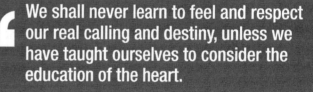

> **We shall never learn to feel and respect our real calling and destiny, unless we have taught ourselves to consider the education of the heart.**
>
> -Sir Walter Scott

One day during a reading of *Welcome to Merryville* in a kindergarten class, a precocious little boy shouted, "I can see the pictures behind my eyes," just as Peter and Penelope ran in front of Wilbur and Tommy in the story. First grade girls wanted to know Bonnie Butterfly's colors. On another day, a second-grader said she could smell chocolate chip cookies baking in Mrs. McDonald's oven! Third-graders often want to share their ideas about how Tommy can help Bully.

Young or not-so-young, every soul longs for Merryville. We hope *you*, and your students, enjoy Merryville as much as we enjoy bringing it to you.

Big Ideas

- Defining manners as an attitude of the heart that is self-giving not self-serving, manners are not a set of rules to be followed, but rather principles that guide behavior.
- Manners are the foundation for morals.

Grade-level skills and objectives

(K) Children are introduced to the characters of Merryville and find ways they can have hearts like Tommy's.

(1) Children are introduced to the characters of Merryville and find ways to show what is in their hearts.

(2) Children are introduced to the characters of Merryville and find the characters in Merryville to be just like them.

(3) Children are introduced to the characters of Merryville and learn why bullies bully.

Manners in Merryville

Materials and Preparation

- "Welcome to Merryville" (found at the end of the lesson)
- Wise Ol' Wilbur, Peter and Penelope puppets
- Copies of "Map of Merryville" (1/student)
- Coloring utensils

Wilbur's Words of Wisdom

Manners come from the heart.

Guiding Children's Learning

In today's lesson, we introduce your students to the characters of Merryville to begin their process of understanding manners.

Begin by introducing the Wise Ol' Wilbur, Peter and Penelope puppets.

Attributes
Manners in the Heart

Kindergarten Skills and Objectives:

Children are introduced to the characters of Merryville and find ways they can have a heart full of manners. In this lesson, children will learn the following:
- Manners come from a good heart.
- Manners help you make friends.

Explain that in today's story we're going to visit the town of Merryville where Wise Ol' Wilbur and his friends live. Use the map of Merryville to help ignite your students' imaginations. Encourage them to listen to the story with their hearts—their imaginations. Remind them they can 'see' the characters if they'll look with the eyes of their hearts.

Read "Welcome to Merryville" with great enthusiasm and animation!

After the reading, lead the children in a discussion about Merryville and the characters they meet in the story. Use the questions and answers below as a guide. Encourage the children to give their own answers first.

Where is Merryville?
- *Between the mountains and the sea*

What happened to Tommy at the beginning of the story?

- *He rode his bike too fast down a steep hill and crashed into a mailbox under a giant tree*

Who lives in the giant tree?

- *Wise Ol' Wilbur*

Do you think Wilbur is wise? Why?

- *He knows everyone in town.*
- *He is old.*
- *He cares about all the critters.*
- *He knows A LOT.*

Is Tommy a nice boy with good manners?

- *Yes*

How do you know that Tommy has good manners?

- *He apologizes to Wilbur for running into his mailbox.*
- *Tommy says, "Sir" to Wilbur.*
- *Tommy says, "Thank you" to Wilbur.*
- *He pats PD on the head.*
- *Tommy heads home without a fuss when Wilbur reminds him it is time.*
- *He wants to help Bully.*

Where do Tommy's manners come from?

- *His heart!*

Now, ask the children if Tommy makes new friends by using good manners. Tell the children they're going to learn a lot about good manners throughout the year.

To close, share three reasons why using manners, like Tommy, is important:

1. Children with good manners help others.
2. It's easy for children with good manners to make friends.
3. Children with good manners have happy hearts.

|

EXTENDING
CHILDREN'S LEARNING

1. Let your students use the puppets to tell their version of "Welcome to Merryville."

2. Make three copies of the "Manners in Merryville" activity sheet for each student to use in the next three extended learning activities this week. For the first activity, ask your students to draw their own picture of Merryville as they imagine it to be. You could designate one area in your classroom as the "Merryville Art Gallery" to display their work.

3. Ask your students to draw Wilbur's happle tree. Remind them of what they learned about the happle tree from "Welcome to Merryville:"

   - It's gigantic.
   - It stands in a bend in the road on the way to Merryville.
   - The leaves are a hundred shades of green.
   - There are bright red balls that look like giant heart-shaped Christmas ornaments hanging from its branches.
   - A giant red mailbox stands underneath the tree.
   - It's unlike any other tree in the world.

4. Ask your children to draw a picture of Tommy and his friends. When the week is over, send the pictures home with your students.

5. When opportunities arise throughout the year, remind your students to use good manners, like Tommy does. Remind them to show the manners in their hearts by being kind.

Home Connection

Dear Parent/Guardian,

Manners have no social or cultural boundaries. Common courtesy and respect for others should be part of everyday living. *Manners of the Heart* is here to help you help your children become respectful youngsters who grow up to become respectable adults. Defining manners as an attitude of the heart that is self-giving not self-serving teaches children to respect others, and in the process, learn to respect themselves. Through storytelling, hands-on activities, and role play, your child will learn the importance of manners, and so much more, this school year.

Each week, your child will bring you a **Home Connection** page. This is your recommended homework, which we call "Heartwork." It is our belief that you're the one who holds the key to unlock your child's heart so the mind will open to all he or she can learn in the classroom and at home. We hope you can make time to do one or more of the suggested activities during the week to reinforce the lessons your child is receiving at school. We assure you, you'll enjoy the time with your child, and even more, your child will enjoy the time spent with you. Working together, we can help your child become all that he or she is meant to be.

This week, we're introducing your child to Merryville, a fictional town, where Wise Ol' Wilbur and his friends live. Through the story of Merryville, your child is learning that manners come from the heart. Ask your child to tell you the story of Merryville tonight!

~ From Our Hearts To Yours

Map of Merryville

Manners in Merryville

WELCOME
TO MERRYVILLE

Tommy Tripper and his family just moved outside a quiet little town nestled between the mountains and the sea called Merryville. After days of unpacking boxes, Tommy asked his mom if he could explore their new town.

Before she could finish saying yes, Tommy hopped on his bike and sped down the steep hill into Merryville. He came around a bend in the road much too fast. He lost control of his bike and slid into a big red mailbox under a gigantic tree. Tommy was dazed. For a little bit, the only thing he could see was stars before his eyes. When his head cleared, the stars faded, revealing a tree, unlike any other tree he had ever seen.

The leaves were a hundred shades of green, and there were bright red balls that looked like giant heart-shaped Christmas ornaments hanging from the branches. As Tommy stood up to take a closer look, he heard a voice from high in the treetop, "Whooooo goes there?"

Tommy looked up to see an enormous old owl looking down at him. The owl's eyebrows reminded him of the handlebars on his bike. The owl's eyes were turquoise blue like the color of the sea. His bright yellow beak stood so far out from his face that Tommy wondered how the owl kept from falling over when he talked.

The owl called again, "I said, whooooo goes there?"

"It's Tommy," the boy said.

Wilbur left his perch and swooped down to his big red mailbox. He saw that Tommy was not hurt, and he asked, "Tommy whooooo?"

"Tommy Tripper, sir," replied the boy.

"Tommy Tripper. It's mighty nice to meet you," said the owl. "I'm Wise Ol' Wilbur. But most folks call me Wilbur for short. You're new in town, aren't you?"

"Yes, sir. That was my first ride down the hill. I'm sorry I ran into your mailbox. I'll have to be more careful next time," said Tommy.

"Well, you're not the first kid to run into my mailbox, and you probably won't be the last," said Wilbur, as he polished the shiny red box with his wing. "Would you like me to show you around town?"

"I sure would, Wilbur. Thank you," replied Tommy.

"Well, then, let's head on down the hill past the pond by Mrs. McDonald's house." As they passed the pond, Tommy heard a frog croaking joyfully. Wilbur said, "That's

| **25**

Freddie the Frog. He's always in a good mood."

As they approached the big yellow house, Wilbur said, "Mrs. McDonald lives there. She is one of the nicest ladies around. She makes the best cookies in town."

Tommy looked at the big yellow house with a pretty yard filled with flowers. He wondered if Mrs. McDonald baked his favorite cookies.

Tommy and Wilbur continued their walk. Suddenly, two raccoons scurried across in front of them. "That's Peter and Penelope. They're twins," said Wilbur, as he dove in front of Tommy to keep him from tripping over the furry little animals. "Penelope can think a bit too much of herself sometimes. Peter has a good heart. He tries really hard to be good."

While Tommy was watching Peter and Penelope turn the corner by the bake shop, he smelled something that didn't smell like fresh-baked goodies. "Ugh, what's that stink, Wilbur?" asked Tommy.

"Must be Sketch," answered Wilbur.

"Who's Sketch?" asked Tommy.

"Sketch is a pesky skunk who loves to raise a big stink. He's a real trouble-maker. People run when they see him coming."

"I don't blame 'em. He *really* stinks," said Tommy. "Can we move a little faster, Wilbur?"

"Sure thing, Tommy," answered Wilbur.

"Look, there's PD the puppy dog and KC the kitty cat on the other side of the street."

Tommy ran across the street to meet the little white puppy dog covered with black spots. Prancing next to him was a big yellow kitty cat with a big attitude that matched his big head.

As Tommy patted PD, he heard a loud bumblebee overhead. "That's BillyBeeRight," said Wilbur. "He buzzes wildly when somebody's about to do the wrong thing. I suspect there's trouble ahead."

Sure enough, Bully the Bulldog was coming down the street. "Bully likes to hurt people's feelings," said Wilbur. "He does mean things because he has a mean heart. He saw PD getting all the attention and wanted it for himself. BillyBeeRight is trying to stop him, but Bully isn't listening."

Bully chased PD away with a mean growl. "I hate it when Bully acts like a bully," Wilbur said.

While PD ran for cover, Bully came up to Tommy for a pat on *his* head. Tommy looked down at Bully, but didn't pet him.

26 |

Bully's heart turned from mad to sad.

"Bully, when are you going to learn? No one will help you if you hurt others," said another bulldog who walked up behind Tommy.

The second bulldog introduced himself. "I'm Buddy. I try to help Bully, but most of the time he can't hear me because his heart is locked up tight."

Tommy looked at Bully and then back at Buddy with a puzzled look. He said, "You look just like Bully."

"That's right," Wilbur said, "but Buddy has a white spot on his chest shaped like a heart. One day, we're hoping Bully will have one, too."

"This is Tommy, the new kid in town," said Wilbur to Buddy.

"Nice to meet you, Tommy. I'm sorry you saw Bully being a bully," said Buddy. "We're trying to change his heart. Maybe you'll be able to help us."
Just then, Wilbur noticed the sun was going down.

"You better head home, Tommy," Wilbur said. "It will be dark soon, and your mom will be worried. Tomorrow will be another day in Merryville."

Tommy hopped back on his bike and waved to his new friends.

Tommy found out that going up the steep hill was even harder than coming down. On the way home, Tommy thought about Bully's sad heart.

Maybe tomorrow I can help Buddy help Bully. Maybe together we can help his sad heart turn glad.

JUST THE BEGINNING...

Part 1   Attitudes of the Heart

Chapter 1

Helping Others

We all know and love the children's classic, *How the Grinch Stole Christmas*. Living on snowy Mount Crumpit just north of Whoville, the Grinch spends his days concocting a dastardly scheme to ruin Christmas for the Whos. After analyzing reasons why the Grinch may hate Christmas so much, Dr. Seuss gives the most out-of-the-ordinary reason:

> It could be his head wasn't screwed on just right.
> It could be, perhaps, that his shoes were too tight.
> **But I think that the most likely reason of all**
> **May have been that his heart was two sizes too small.**

Could the explanation for the Grinch's 'bullying' of the Whos be this simple? That "his heart was two sizes too small?" At Manners of the Heart®, we believe this is the reason for the Grinch's struggles and your students' struggles, too. From bullying to laziness. From selfishness to entitlement. Hearts that are too small. Hearts locked from the emptiness of poverty or the overindulgence of privilege.

The answer to your students' struggles is unlocking their hearts to open their minds to all you have to teach them. The first turn of the key is helping them experience the joy of helping others. With each act of goodwill, you'll watch your students' hearts grow. As their hearts grow, their minds will open.

After the Grinch accomplishes his goal of robbing the Whos of all symbols of Christmas, he stands at the peak of Mount Crumpit to send the sleigh full of Christmas cheer over the cliff. But rather than hearing the cry of empty-hearted Whos, he hears singing and celebration from hearts full of the 'right' stuff.

> And what happened then? Well, in Whoville they say
> that **the Grinch's small heart grew three sizes that day.**
> And then the true meaning of Christmas came through,
> and the Grinch found the strength of ten Grinches, plus two!

In an instant, his heart fills with kindness and love, transforming the Grinch from a criminal to a hero. He spends the rest of his days as part of the Whoville family. His outward expressions of kindness reflect the inward condition of his love-filled heart. He finally becomes all he is meant to be.

Like the Grinch, a young pirate finds a new heart after a storm tosses his chest full of gold overboard. Coming ashore in Merryville he discovers real treasure that lasts the rest of the days of his life.

Your students can find real treasure, too, when they discover the joy that comes from helping others instead of themselves.

30 |

Big Ideas

- When we teach children to put the needs of others ahead of their wants, their hearts will grow. As their hearts grow, their minds open.
- Acts of kindness and love help children develop others-centeredness, enabling them to become valuable members of their community.
- Helping others makes the world a better place.

Grade-level skills and objectives:

(K) Children learn the joy of helping by fulfilling their duties for the good of the family.

(1) Looking for ways to help others in their neighborhood and in their school teaches your students how to look at others with the eyes of their hearts.

(2) With each act of goodwill to others, the hearts of your students unlock to the possibilities around them.

(3) Developing the ability to put the needs of others ahead of their wants, your students learn the joy of being a "helping hand."

Helping At Home

Materials and Preparation

Optional Items:
- Copies of "Here We Go 'Round the Happle Tree" (1 for you or 1/student)
- Laundry basket
- Assorted pieces of clothing and/or towels
- A few toys from your learning center
- Your students' shoes

Wilbur's Words of Wisdom

Let's do our duties on one, two, three…
It's time to help our family!

Guiding Children's Learning

In today's lesson, students will begin to understand they each have a critical role to play at home. As a member of a family, they have a duty to help keep their home in order. By helping at home, children show great love for their family. (And remember, if your students develop a sense of duty as a member of the family, it is easy to transition this idea to their role in the classroom!)

(Optional—As you prepare for today's lesson, scatter the assorted pieces of clothing, shoes, toys, and towels around the room.)

Begin the lesson by asking your students the following questions:

- Do you have chores to do at home?
- Do you like doing your chores?
- Do you have to be reminded to do your chores?
- When you're reminded, do you do them right away or do you put off doing your chores?

Now, tell the children they're going to practice helping others while learning a fun song about doing duties.

Attributes

Kindness, Love

Kindergarten Skills and Objectives:

Children learn the joy of helping by fulfilling their duties for the good of the family. In this lesson, children will learn the following:
- To do their part as a member of a family
- To pick up their toys to keep others from tripping over them
- To put dirty clothes in the laundry basket

Using the song lyrics for "Here We Go 'Round the Happle Tree" (to the tune of "Here We Go 'Round the Mulberry Bush"), instruct several children to act out the verses of the song as they sing. For instance, while singing, "This is the way we hang our clothes," the children will pick up a piece of clothing and hang it on their coat hook. While singing, "This is the way we place our shoes," the children will pick up their shoes and place them in their cubby. While singing, "This is the way we pick up towels," the children will pick up a towel and put it in the laundry basket, and so on. (You can also choose to have students pretend to act out the different verses of the song if you don't have the props.)

Sing the song a few more times while acting silly to make the 'chores' fun for the kids.

Encourage your students to keep up the good work at home! (One study out of the University of Minnesota showed that children who did housework had better feelings of responsibility and self-worth years later.)[1]

If time allows, choose one or more of the **Extended Learning** activities.

Close with the following comments:

- Doing your chores without complaining is a great way to show your helpfulness to your family.
- Last week, you learned about the town of Merryville and its many characters. You were told to remember your manners, like Tommy did, and helping others is one very important way to show the manners that are in your heart.
- I want to see you helping others here in the classroom, too—not just at home!
- There will always be opportunities to help others. You just have to be paying attention.

1 "Involving Children in Household Tasks: Is It Worth It?" by Dr Marty Rossman, Found online at: http://www.cehd.umn.edu/ research/highlights/Rossmann/

Definitions:

KINDNESS
Showing care and consideration in an unexpected and exceptional way

LOVE
Genuinely caring for another, unconditionally

EXTENDING
CHILDREN'S LEARNING

1. Help your students remember to do their duties for their family, using the "Duty Chart." Give each child a copy of the chart. Explain that they will bring the chart home to use. Parents can fill in the duties they want their child to complete. As a duty is completed, they should color in the space under the day it was completed. Students may bring the chart back to school in a week to share how they helped their families.

2. Read *The Berenstain Bears and the Trouble With Chores* by Jan & Mike Berenstain (HarperFestival, 2005). Explain that in today's story we're going to find that the Bears don't like to do their chores either, but they find out that not doing their chores causes too much trouble! After the reading, lead the children in a discussion about what happens at the Bears' house when no one does their chores. Use the questions below as a guide:

   - Do the Bears like doing chores?
   - Do Brother and Sister Bear fuss with each other about doing chores?
   - Why does Mama Bear want the cubs to do their chores?
   - Are the Bears happy when the chores don't get done?
   - Do you think Brother and Sister learn a lesson about doing their part to keep their home clean and neat?

3. Read "The Watchman of Merryville" (found at the end of the lesson). Make the following points to your students:

   - Just as the eyes of Cap'n Nick's heart open to helping Ol' McDonald instead of *hurting* him, the eyes of other people's hearts can open, too.
   - Look for ways to help others this week.
   - Remember, the more you help others, the bigger their hearts grow.
   - The more you help others, the bigger your heart grows.
   - The bigger your heart grows, the more you will want to help others.

4. When leaving for lunch or another activity, ask the children to let someone go ahead of them in line. When they return, let them take turns holding the door open for each other. Look for other opportunities for students to exercise their helpfulness to you, classmates, or other students or adults in the school.

5. Using family magazines, have your students make a "Helping Others" poster for your classroom. Throughout the week, have students cut out pictures from magazines that depict people helping each other. Let the children use a glue stick to add their pictures to the poster. With each addition, allow the child to explain why he or she selected the picture.

Home Connection

Dear Parent/Guardian,

This week, Manners of the Heart® is reminding children of the importance of fulfilling their duties at home. Kindergartners are learning the following:

- To do their part as a member of a family
- To pick up their toys to keep others from tripping over them
- To put dirty clothes in the laundry basket

Here are a few ways to support your child's helpfulness at home:

- **Give your child regular duties and hold him or her accountable for taking care of those duties.** Children need to experience being a part of something greater than themselves. When you give your child duties that only they perform, your child experiences the satisfaction of having something of value to contribute to the family. (Notice that we use the term *duty* rather than *chore*. A **chore** *tends to become a task that a parent gives a child to relieve the parent of the burden. A **duty** is for the child's sake; it's for the purpose of teaching the child to be responsible and to find fulfillment in a job well done.)*

- **Assign duties that have a purpose.** No matter the age of your child, any duties you assign them should have one or more of the following intentions:

    - Helping your child learn life skills
    - Helping your child become a valuable member of the family
    - Helping your child become a valuable member of society

- **Assign duties that are age-appropriate.** Are you wondering what duties to give your kindergartner? The goal is to help your child find satisfaction in accomplishing simple tasks. Young children have a strong desire to please. You can build on that desire by allowing them to help you. Here are a few age-appropriate duties:

    - Five-year-olds are capable of organizing their room or "space" to accommodate their belongings. Walk your children through the process of
      picking up their toys and placing them in the proper place.
    - Kindergartners are also very capable of putting away their shoes and putting dirty clothes in the laundry hamper.

~ From Our Hearts To Yours

Here We Go Round the Happle Tree

Here we go 'round the happle tree
The happle tree, the happle tree
Here we go 'round the happle tree
So early in the morning.

This is the way we hang our clothes
Hang our clothes, hang our clothes
This is the way we hang our clothes
So early Monday morning.

This is the way we place our shoes
Place our shoes, place our shoes
This is the way we place our shoes
So early Tuesday morning.

This is the way we pick up towels
Pick up towels, pick up towels
This is the way we pick up towels
So early Wednesday morning.

This is the way we pick up toys
Pick up toys, pick up toys
This is the way we pick up toys
So early Thursday morning.

This is the way we sweep the floor
Sweep the floor, sweep the floor
This is the way we sweep the floor
So early Friday morning.

This is the way we clean our rooms
Clean our rooms, clean our rooms
This is the way we clean our rooms
So early Saturday morning.

This is the way we help at home
Help at home, help at home
This is the way we help at home
So early Sunday morning.

DUTY CHART

Duties:	Sunday	Monday	Tuesday	Wednes- day	Thursday	Friday	Saturday

| **37**

PART 1

THE WATCHMAN
OF MERRYVILLE

It was a beautiful day in Merryville when, suddenly, clouds started moving in from the sea. The winds blew strong. Big waves crashed on the rocks. The sky became dark, even though it was the middle of the day. Ol' Farmer McDonald, who had lived in Merryville all his born days, knew this was a storm like no other he had ever seen. He jumped in his old truck and headed for the lighthouse to take a closer look.

When he got to the top of the lighthouse, he looked out over the sea and saw a giant tornado in the distance, roaring over the water toward Merryville. Far from the shore, he could see a ship being tossed about in the waves. He climbed into the tower to ring its big brass bell, alerting the people of Merryville of the coming storm.

Ol' McDonald jumped back in his truck and rushed to his farm to nail down the shutters on his windows. Folks along the way hollered their thank you's to Ol' McDonald for sounding the alarm as they headed for cover. Bully and Buddy scurried down the road toward their home. Peter and Penelope saw everyone running, so they started running, too!

Ol' McDonald was right. This was the worst storm ever to hit Merryville. Rain came down in buckets. Freddie the Frog

tried to ride out the storm on his lily pad, but it was too much for him. He hopped into the water to get out of the wind. Lightning lit the sky all around. Winds blew into the night.

Just after dark, Sketch peeked out from his hollowed-out tree trunk to see the tornado pass high in the sky, sparing Merryville. By morning, the sky was clear. The winds were calm. The birds sang their songs. The sun shone brightly. Wilbur, the wise old owl, came out of his Happle Tree and called out, "Whooooo, Wee! What a night!"

Townspeople came out to check on their neighbors. Everyone seemed to be all right, but Merryville was a mess. Tree limbs were down everywhere. Ol' McDonald came out to begin picking up pieces around his yard. He wondered about the ship he had seen during the storm and who might have been on it.

Wilbur flew down from the Happle Tree to check on him, when he saw someone go into Ol' McDonald's barn. "Whooooo goes there?" Wilbur called. Ol' McDonald was startled when he saw someone moving around in his barn.

He headed to the barn to see who was there. To his surprise, he saw a barefoot young man who was soaking wet like he had just climbed out of the sea. He had a black scarf tied on his head, an earring in his ear, and an old-looking key tied on a leather cord around his neck. When the young man heard Wilbur call, he hid his sack full of stolen loot behind a stack of hay bales. Ol' McDonald knew this young man must be a pirate from the ship he had seen being tossed at sea only the night before.

"You look like you could use a hot meal. I was just about to cook some eggs and bacon for breakfast. Would you like to join me?"asked Ol' McDonald. Without a smile or a thank-you, the young man said he would join him.

This was the first time in this young pirate's life anyone had ever been so kind to him.

The two men talked while they ate breakfast. The young pirate told Ol' McDonald his name was Nicholas, and he was able to save his own life by getting a small boat off the ship and paddling to shore just before the ship sank. It was dark when he made it to the shore, so he stayed in the boat and waited for the storm to pass.

Ol' McDonald never asked Nicholas why he was in his barn, but he offered the young pirate a set of dry clothes and a new pair of shoes. The young man changed his clothes and put on his new shoes. He then headed back toward town, still without thanking Ol' McDonald.

There was plenty of work in town after the storm. Nicholas worked for different folks during the day and came back to steal from them at night. BillyBeeRight tried with all his might to stop him. He buzzed 'round and round' Nicholas's head every time he began stuffing his bag with more loot. Nicholas ignored him and kept adding to his stash behind the hay bales.

After a week, he knew he had better move on or he would get caught. He heard the weekly train blow its whistle and knew this would be his only escape. He threw his bag of loot on top of a stack of feed sacks in the back of Ol' McDonald's truck and headed for the station. Just as he drove past Ol' McDonald's bean field, Nicholas heard Chester barking like a crazy dog. He looked over to see Chester standing next to Ol' McDonald, who was lying by the road.

Nicholas knew if he stopped to help him, he would miss the train. But something strange was happening in Nicholas's heart. For the first time in his life, Nicholas thought about someone other than himself. He slammed on the brakes and jumped out of the truck. He ran to Ol' McDonald and found a great big knot on the side of the old man's head. The last thing Ol' McDonald remembered was that a mouse spooked his horse, and he fell to the ground.

Nicholas put Ol' McDonald in the truck and drove straight to Dr. Feltbetter's office. As it turned out, Ol' McDonald's head was okay, but his right arm was broken and had to be put in a cast. The word spread like wildfire through town that Ol' McDonald had been hurt. Bully and Buddy, Penelope and Peter, and KC, the kitty cat, all crowded in front of Dr. Feltbetter's window worried about their dear old friend.

When Dr. Feltbetter finished wrapping Ol' McDonald's arm, Nicholas took him back to the farm and tucked him in bed. He sat next to his bed all night long. The next morning, he fed the kind old man breakfast and started doing chores around the farm. With each kindness, his heart grew. The more he helped, the bigger his heart became.

At night, rather than stealing again, he returned the goods he had stolen. Every time he took something back, his heart grew more. Soon, he found himself wanting to help others rather than hurting them.

However; he still had the things he had stolen from Ol' McDonald. In the morning after breakfast, he took a deep breath and told Ol' McDonald the truth.

"When I was in the storm at sea," Nicholas said, "the waves were so high that my treasure chest full of gold washed overboard. I came into Merryville to steal as much as I had lost. The day you found me in your barn, I was stealing from you, but you were kind to me. You gave me food and clothing. You taught me that giving is better than taking. For the first time in my life, I felt a part of something good. All I want to do with the rest of my life is to help others like you helped me."

"I know just the job for you," answered Ol' McDonald. They headed into town to see the Mayor of Merryville, who agreed Nicholas was the right man to watch over Merryville.
The very next day, all the townsfolk

gathered at the lighthouse. Sitting on the rocks at the shore, Buddy and Bully, KC and PD, and Peter and Penelope all watched as the Mayor gave Nicholas the key to the lighthouse and his new title, "Cap'n Nick, the Watchman of Merryville."

To this day, he lives in the lighthouse by the sea and watches over Merryville by day and by night.

JUST THE BEGINNING...

Chapter 2

Excusing Others and Excusing Me

Do you become frustrated by the behaviors of other drivers on the roads? At the grocery, does it annoy you when the person in line in front of you is not paying attention to the open counter? Or, are you more likely the person who feels rushed—or even harassed—by the short-tempered person driving or standing behind you?

Many times, we are quick to judge the behaviors of others, yet slow to recognize our own faults. As adults, we know others have different abilities, talents, attributes, perspectives or personalities from our own; yet, it is often hard to remember these differences and even harder to actually appreciate them. However; it is the combination of our differences that enables our families, classrooms, and communities to grow. An important part of living with others involves learning how to excuse the faults of others while also asking others to excuse ours.

In these lessons, children learn how and why to use apologies and exercise forgiveness. By forgiving or excusing others, children develop *patience* to accept the differences or faults of others. By asking for forgiveness when needed, children also learn *humility*, a quality that is much more about how we treat others than what we think of ourselves. A child with a patient and humble heart will be able to both give and receive forgiveness.

Big Ideas

- Children can't succeed socially or emotionally unless they learn patience in excusing the faults of others.
- Children cultivate humility in asking for forgiveness when they are at fault.

Grade-level skills and objectives:

(K) Children learn how to exercise patience with others.

(1) Children learn to right their wrong by saying "I'm sorry."

(2) Children learn to be quick to forgive and quick to ask for forgiveness.

(3) Children learn that forgiveness is not only about helping the person who hurt you to feel better— forgiveness is also about letting go of those bad feelings inside.

Wait, Wait, Wait

Materials and Preparation

- "The Tortoise and the Skunk" (found at the end of the lesson)
- Wise Ol' Wilbur puppet

Wilbur's Words of Wisdom

To patiently *wait* is something just *great!*

Not now, not now,
I have to wait.
I'll wait for now,
Then, wait and wait.

Guiding Children's Learning

Begin by reading "The Tortoise and the Skunk."

Using Wilbur, lead a discussion with the children about the meaning of the story:

Wilbur: Is it Henry's fault that he is slow? Or is he just different from Sketch?
- *Just different*

Wilbur: "Do you think Sketch is very nice to Henry?"
- *No, he is not very nice at all!*

Wilbur: "How do you think Sketch makes Henry feel when he runs ahead?"
- *Like he is less important than Sketch*
- *Like Sketch does not like him or care about him*

Wilbur: "Do you think Sketch is patient with Henry? Why not?"
- *No, he does not wait for him.*
- *No, he is rude about Henry being slow.*

Wilbur: "Do you ever feel frustrated when you have to wait for someone? Let's talk about sometimes when you may feel frustrated for waiting."
- *I feel frustrated when the teacher is passing out snacks, and I have to wait!*

Attributes

Humility, Patience

Kindergarten Skills and Objectives:

Patience is the foundation of excusing and forgiving others. In this lesson, kindergartners will learn that being patient is important, because of the following:
- We all have to wait at different times.
- Being impatient with others makes them feel unimportant.
- We like when others are patient with us so we need to be patient with them.

- *When I want to go to my friend's house, but I have to wait for Mom to take me*
- *When I have to wait for the bus to come*
- *When I have to wait for mom to get her hair done*
- *When I have to wait for Evelyn to finish with the blue crayon*
- *When I'm riding my bike, and I have to wait for my sister to catch up*
- *When I have to wait for my turn on the slide*
- *When I have to wait for the teacher to call on me*

Definitions:

HUMILITY
Not caring who gets credit

PATIENCE
Even-tempered endurance

Wilbur: "What does it mean to be *patient?*"
- *To wait for others to have their turn*
- *To wait for others who are slower than you*
- *To be nice while you are waiting*

Wilbur: "You probably like it when others are patient with you, right? It's no fun when someone is hurrying you or making you feel slow. So it is important to remember to be patient with others, too.

Here's a rhyme to help you be patient when you have to wait:

Not now, not now,
I have to wait.
I'll wait for now,
Then, wait and wait.

Say it with me this time. The next time you have to wait, but don't want to, say this little rhyme to help you be patient."

Close by repeating the rhyme several times until the students can remember it. Tell them both you and Wilbur will be looking for boys and girls who use patience this week!

EXTENDING
CHILDREN'S LEARNING

1. Buy some seeds, dirt and a container for the children to participate in the process of growing something special in your classroom. They will need to take turns watering it and giving it fertilizer. This ongoing activity will be a special way for your students to better understand the long-term reward of exercising patience. It will be very exciting for them to see the flower or grass begin to grow!

2. Help your students practice being patient by playing a new version of "Freeze." Tell your class, "We're going to practice our patience today by playing 'Freeze.' You can wiggle and giggle until I say 'freeze'; then you have to stand as still as a statue and not make a sound, until I tag you. If I don't tag you, you CANNOT move. You have to wait for me to get to you. If you can't wait till I get to you, you're out of the game!" Tag your students who exhibit the most patience first! As the kids are tagged, they can cheer on their classmates to wait!

3. Kindergartners are accustomed to completing a story during one sitting. This week, choose a chapter book and read a aloud few pages each day during naptime or reading time. This helps your students develop patience because they know they have to wait until the next day for the rest of the story. One of the books from Arthur's Chapter Book Series (such as *Arthur's Mystery Envelope*) would be a great choice.

4. Here are some simple opportunities to reinforce patience in your kindergartners:

   - Require children to always say "Please" and "Thank you" first before eating a treat.
   - Have children take turns being at the front of the line.
   - When a child is being impatient in line, have him or her move to the back of the line to try again.
   - During snack time, teach children the table etiquette rule of waiting until everyone has been served before eating (TIP—Manners of the Heart® has a table manners curriculum, *At the Table*, that teaches children additional ways to practice patience at meals).
   - Require children to raise their hands before speaking in group discussion. Remind them that you can only call on one child at a time and if you are waiting, this is a good opportunity to practice your patience.
   - Encourage kids to quietly say their "Wait" rhyme anytime they feel frustrated with waiting.

Home Connection

Dear Parent/Guardian,

This week, kindergartners are learning about the importance of exercising patience with others. Wilbur is teaching them a rhyme to help them remember to be patient while waiting:

Not now, not now,
I have to wait.
I'll wait for now,
Then, wait and wait.

Here are a few opportunities for you to reinforce patience in your child this week:

1. Talk with your child about the importance of being patient with others. Explain that there is more than one person in your family, and each person has different plans, abilities and personalities. For the family to get along, we have to be patient with each other.

2. Make time for your family to sit down together at the table to practice patience through table manners.

   - Have each family member wait to eat until everyone has been served.
   - Cook difficult foods, such as spaghetti, to teach your children patience as they must work to prepare each bite of food.
   - Teach your child to eat slowly and carefully—no slurping!
   - Teach your children to eat with one hand in their lap, unless he or she is cutting or spreading.

3. At night, read your child a chapter from a classic such as *The Chronicles of Narnia* series. This enables kids to learn the thrill of anticipation, looking forward to the unfolding of the next piece of the story. They learn to wait and use their imaginations in the waiting!

4. Make a point to model patience for your child in the home, in the car and in public.

~ From Our Hearts To Yours

THE TORTOISE
AND THE SKUNK

Once upon a heart in Merryville, there lived a tortoise named Henry, who was traveling through the woods on his way to the pond at Granny's house. All the flowers were in bloom. A soft breeze filled the air with the sweet smell of spring.

Henry stopped to take a deep breath to see if he was getting near the pond. Instead of smelling the pond, however; he got a whiff of something awful. While he was trying to figure out what the stinky smell was, a black and white skunk crossed his path.

They were both surprised. They stopped and looked at each other. Henry said, "I've been in Granny's woods for more years than I can remember, and I've never seen you before. Who are you?"

"I'm Sketch the Skunk, but most people just call me Sketch," answered the skunk.

"Nice to meet you, Sketch. My name is Henry. Everybody just calls me Henry. Do you live around here, Sketch?" asked Henry.

Sketch shook his head and said, "No, I live over by Tripper's Trout Farm. I was just passing through. Where are you going, Henry?"
"I'm going to Granny's pond for a swim," answered Henry.

"Then, I'll go to the pond, too, and have a drink. Do you wanna race?" Sketch asked.

Henry laughed and said, "I used to race a rabbit around here, but I always beat him even though rabbits are supposed to be a lot faster than turtles. Why don't we just go together?"

Sketch said, "Sounds good to me, Henry. Let's go!"

Sketch headed down the trail toward the pond. He turned to say something to Henry, but Henry was nowhere to be seen.

"Henry, where are you?" Sketch called out.

"I'm way back here," Henry hollered back. "I'm not as fast as you."

Sketch said, "I'm really thirsty. Hurry up, Henry. You're just too slow."

"Sketch, I carry my house around with me everywhere I go. I can only move so fast," Henry answered. "You'll just have to be patient and slow down if you want me to keep up with you."

"Okay, Henry. I'll slow down," Sketch said. But in less than five minutes, Sketch snapped at Henry again, "What's taking you so long? Are you just plain lazy?"

"I'll have you know, Sketch the Skunk, I'm not lazy. I can't help it if my legs are short. Why don't you just slow down and smell the flowers along the way?" Henry suggested. "And wait for me."

"Okay," Sketch said.

But less than a minute later, Sketch cried out, "Henry, are you lost? Where are you now?"

"I'm right behind you," Henry answered. "If you can't have patience, just go on without me."

"I'll just do that, you dumb, slow turtle. I'll find my own way to the pond without you. I'm tired of waiting on you," said Sketch as he ran ahead of Henry once again.

Sketch must have forgotten that he didn't know where he was. He kept running until he was just plain lost. He called out for Henry, but there was no answer. The woods looked scary, and it looked like it was going to be getting dark soon.

Meanwhile, Henry kept going slowly and steadily until he made it to the pond, but Sketch wasn't there. He called out for Sketch, but there was no answer. Nightfall came and still no Sketch. Henry was worried now, so he stretched his neck out of his shell and called, "Wilbur, where are you? We need you!"

Suddenly, Wilbur appeared from the sky. He landed on the ground in front of Henry. "Whooooo's in trouble?" Wilbur asked.

"It's Sketch," answered Henry. "He got tired of waiting on me and headed out on his own through the woods, but he doesn't know these woods. I'm worried about him."

"Sit tight, Henry. I'll find him," Wilbur said, as he flew off into the night sky.

With his keen owl eyes, Wilbur saw Sketch hiding in the hollow of a tree. Wilbur thought, *I hope this youngster learned a lesson.* "Sketch, where are you?" Wilbur asked, even though Wilbur knew where he was.

"I'm here, Wilbur," answered Sketch, as he came out of the hollow of the tree.

"Sketch, what are you doing alone in these woods?" Wilbur asked, even though he knew the answer to this question, too.

Sketch explained that he was going to the pond with Henry. "I got tired of waiting on that slow-poke, so I just took off. It's Henry's fault I got lost," whined Sketch.

Wilbur rubbed his ear with his wing, as he always did when he was listening for an answer.

"My dear, Sketch," said Wilbur. "If you had been patient and slowed down for your friend, then you wouldn't have gotten lost. But you chose to be impatient and run ahead without him, and look where it got you."

"I guess I was the dumb one, huh, Wilbur?" asked Sketch.

"Sketch, you were ugly to Henry, don't you think?" Wilbur asked.

"Well, I said some pretty tough things to him," Sketch answered.

"Even so, Henry called me for help because he was worried about you," said Wilbur. "I think you need to tell Henry you're sorry, don't you?"

"Wilbur, will you show me the way to the pond so I can see Henry?" Sketch asked.

"Thought you'd never ask," said Wilbur.

"Just follow me, if you can keep up."

Wilbur flew as fast as he could, circling back and forth. Sketch ran as fast as his little legs would carry him. He knew Wilbur was making sure he'd never forget this lesson.

By the time they made it to the pond, Sketch was thirstier than ever, but when he saw Henry, he ran straight for him, without taking a drink first.

"Sketch, ol' boy," shouted Henry. "I'm so glad you're okay. What happened to you?"

Sketch couldn't believe Henry was glad to see him, after the way he had treated him.

"After I left you, I made a wrong turn at the oak tree in the middle of the woods, and got lost. I should have stayed with you. I'm sorry I didn't have more patience," said Sketch.

Before Sketch could even finish, Henry replied, "That's all right. I understand. I know I'm slow, Sketch, but I do get where I'm going, later or sooner."

"I'm sorry, Henry, for all the mean things I said to you. Will you forgive me?" asked Sketch with a lot of sorrow in his voice.

"I forgive you, Sketch. Now, get yourself a drink. The water is fine," answered Henry.

Henry and Sketch became good friends.

Sketch never gave Henry a hard time about being slow again.

JUST THE BEGINNING...

Chapter

Appreciating Others

Just think how different our world would be "if I think you are more important than I am…. and you think I am more important than you are…and he thinks she is more important than he is… and she thinks he is more important than she is….then in the end, everyone *feels* important but no one *acts* important."[1]

So, if everyone *feels* important but no one *acts* important, then everyone feels appreciated.

In today's society, it seems that most of us fail to make others feel important because we're too busy acting important. We have that mirror syndrome, don't we? Appreciating ourselves rather than appreciating others? The sad thing is, if you live in the mirror long enough, you find the only one who appreciates you is yourself.

Jim Stovall reminds us that we "need to be aware of what others are doing, applaud their efforts, acknowledge their successes, and encourage them in their pursuits. When we all help one another, everybody wins." At Manners of the Heart® we couldn't agree more. We believe we need to help the next generation see beyond themselves to the needs of others.

Manners of the Heart teaches children to appreciate others, to treasure others as more valuable than gold. Kindergartners learn to applaud the accomplishments of others. First-graders experience the joy of sharing with others to show their appreciation for them. When they offer a gift of appreciation to others, second-graders receive the reward of a good heart. Third-graders are reminded of the importance of giving kind words of appreciation and encouragement to others.

In a world that places great value on things and little value on people, we're going to raise the next generation to appreciate people—to add value to the lives of others through their kind words, generous actions and thoughtful deeds.

Now, let's see…if I appreciate you and you appreciate me and we appreciate our students and our students appreciate others…what a wonderful world it will be!

[1] Lucado, Max. *A Love Worth Giving: Living in the Overflow of God's Love.* Nashville, TN: W. Pub. Group, 2002, P. 50. Print.

[2] SearchQuotes.com, Jim Stovall.

PART 1

Big Ideas

- Appreciating others adds value to the lives of those receiving appreciation and to those offering appreciation.
- A child who can freely give compliments to others will become an adult who will add great value to our world.
- Learning to show appreciation for others through kind words and selfless deeds develops humility in a child's heart.

Grade-level skills and objectives:

(K) Children learn the joy of applauding others.

(1) Children experience the joy of sharing their treasure with others.

(2) Children receive the reward of a good heart when they offer a gift of appreciation to others.

(3) Children experience the joy of sharing kind words of appreciation.

Applauding Others

Materials and Preparation

- Copy of the "CHEER" sign (1 total)
- Copy of the "TRY AGAIN" sign (1 total)

(Optional—Print the "CHEER" and "TRY AGAIN" signs on cardstock and glue or tape each to a craft stick)

Wilbur's Words of Wisdom

I'll cheer for you,
You cheer for me—
What a great place
This world can be!

Guiding Children's Learning

In today's lesson, students will play the game of "Classmate Cheer." Here are the steps:

1. Remind the children to stay in their seats as you call out the game questions below.
2. If they know the answer, they should raise their hand and wait to be called on. (This is a good opportunity to remind them of last week's lesson on patiently waiting.)
3. When a student is called on, he or she should stand and give the answer.
4. If they give the correct answer, raise the "CHEER" sign to cue the students to applaud the student with the right answer.
5. If the student gives an incorrect answer, hold up the "TRY AGAIN" sign for students to give their classmate a word of encouragement. If needed, help students come up with encouraging things to say (e.g., "Good try!" or "You'll get it next time!").
6. If the student gives an incorrect answer, he or she should sit back down and try again next time.

Here are the questions for the game (choose as many as you like):

- Who is the Wise Old Owl? (Wise Ol' Wilbur)
- Who is Penelope's brother? (Peter the Raccoon)
- Who raises a stink in Merryville? (Sketch the Skunk)
- Who has eyebrows like handlebars? (Wilbur the Wise Ol' Owl)
- What is the first letter of Merryville? (M)
- Who buzzes around kids to keep them out of trouble? (BillyBeeRight)

Attributes

Appreciation, Encouragement

Kindergarten Skills and Objectives:

Learning to applaud others helps children appreciate the accomplishments of others. In this lesson, children will learn the following:

- How to congratulate others for a job well done
- How to give words of encouragement to others who fail
- How to appreciate the efforts of others

- Who is new to Merryville? (Tommy)
- Who is the bulldog with a heart on his chest? (Buddy)
- What kind of tree does Wilbur live in? (A Happle Tree)
- What color is the mailbox under Wilbur's tree? (Red)
- What kind of animal is slow Henry? (A tortoise)
- Who is too fast for Henry? (Sketch the Skunk)
- A couple weeks ago, we sang: "Here we go round the_____." (Happle Tree)

> **Definitions:**
>
> ***APPRECIATION***
> Recognizing and acknowledging value in people, places and things
>
> ***ENCOURAGEMENT***
> Offering words to others to build their confidence

Teach students **Wilbur's Words of Wisdom**, and then close with the following comments:

- I enjoyed seeing you cheer for and encourage your classmates today.
- You will always have the opportunity to say kind things that make people feel good whether they win or lose.
- It makes us feel good when others *appreciate* our efforts by cheering for us or by encouraging us.
- This week, Wilbur and I want to see boys and girls who applaud and encourage others!

EXTENDING
CHILDREN'S LEARNING

1. Reinforce this week's lesson by teaching your students "Cheering for You" to the tune of "London Bridge is Falling Down." Divide your students into pairs. Stand them facing each other as they sing the tune and act out the motions with their partner.

CHEERING FOR YOU

Cheering for you
Just for you   (Clap, clap, clap)
Just for you   (Clap, clap, clap)
Just for you   (Clap, clap, clap)
Cheering for you
Just for you   (Clap, clap, clap)
My dear fri-end

Bowing to you
Just to you (Bow to friend)
Just to you (Bow to friend)
Just to you (Bow to friend)
Bowing to you
Just to you (Bow to friend)
My dear fri-end

2. Read "Tommy's Treasure" to your class. Point out how Tommy encourages others in Merryville by sharing his treasure with them!

3. Tell your students to ask an adult or an older sibling who they like to cheer for (e.g., an athlete, politician, etc.). Lead a discussion with your class on all the different people who are applauded and why it might be important for these people to feel appreciated by the cheers of fans.

4. Write the word "CHEER" on the whiteboard, using the acronym below. Using a different letter for each day of the week, encourage your students to use that action or phrase to encourage others!!

Can do it

High Five

Excellent job

Especially great

Right on

Home Connection

Dear Parent/Guardian,

This week, students are learning the value of appreciating others. Kindergartners are engaged in the opportunity to cheer for classmates by learning the following:

- To congratulate others for a job well done
- To give words of encouragement to others who fail
- To appreciate the efforts of others

Kindergartners are also learning Wilbur's cheer poem:

> I'll cheer for you,
> You cheer for me—
> What a great place
> This world can be!

The most powerful way to reinforce your child's development of appreciation involves modeling appreciative behavior. Here are some of our ideas:

- Say "Thank you" to your child.
- Thank service providers—from clerks to bank tellers to the paper boy.
- Show appreciation for simple pleasures, such as good health, creation, kindness, a good night's rest, a good meal, etc.
- Show love and appreciation to your spouse. Say "Thank you" for small kindnesses and expect your children to respect your spouse.
- Don't complain about minor annoyances or about wanting things you don't have.
- When you are contemplating a purchase, ask if the item is really something you (or a family member) need, or if the item is something you want.
- Display good manners.
- Take turns with your child giving and receiving compliments. Just be silly with it. The point is to help your child develop the habit of offering encouraging words to others.
- Always acknowledge your child when he or she enters a room.
- Send your child a written "Thank you" for an exceptional task completed.
- Watch your child's favorite television show with him or her.
- Try not to miss any event your child participates in.
- Hug, hug, hug.

Watching appreciation of others in action is the best way for your child to learn how to do it themselves!

~ From Our Hearts To Yours

CHEER!

CHEER!

PART 1

TOMMY'S
TREASURE

Tommy loved to spend his days walking along the seashore in Merryville looking for treasure. Day after day he collected seashells, shark teeth, starfish, and sand dollars. One day, the bright sunlight revealed a shiny gold coin in the sand. He looked around to see if anyone was watching. There was no one in sight, so he reached down and picked it up.

The coin looked to be old, much older than he. When he looked at the face on the coin, it appeared the face looked back at him.

Tommy's heart began to pound as his mind raced with possibilities.

Where did the coin come from?
Could there be more coins buried in the sand?
What if there were a treasure chest nearby filled with gold coins?

The sun began setting, so Tommy held the coin tightly in his hand and headed home, telling no one about his discovery. He tossed and turned all night. He couldn't stop thinking about all the possibilities that awaited him the next morning.

The sun was just above the horizon when he left the breakfast table and headed to the beach for another day of searching for treasure. Today was even better than the day before. It seemed everywhere he looked, he found another coin and another and another. He finally had to go home to find a bucket to carry them all!

He hid his coins in the back of his closet. Again, he tossed and turned all night. He couldn't wait to go back to the beach for another day of collecting coins, but this time he would go prepared. He would take his book bag with him to put the coins in so he could keep them safe.

During the night, a storm blew in, bringing an extra high tide. The surf washed all kinds of stuff up on the sand…seaweed and bottles, old boots and cans. The more Tommy searched, the more junk he found. Suddenly, he saw a flash of light in the surf. He combed through the sand to find another coin. When he reached down for the coin, he stumped his toe on a wooden box about the size of a shoe box.

Knowing it was something special, he picked it up, carrying it back onto the beach. He set it down into the sand before looking back down at the waves, noticing a trail of coins behind him. He quickly walked back, picking up the coins and putting them in his pockets before running back to the box. Tommy looked around making sure that no one was around before kneeling in front of the old wooden box.

On the front of the water-worn wood was a rusty lock. As he reached out to touch it, it broke into his hand. Tommy felt his heart quicken with excitement as he pondered the mystery behind this box. His hands shook as he reached out, lifting the lid and revealing that the box was full of gold coins! A treasure chest! Tommy had never seen such a sight! Scared that someone might find it, he packed up all his things and put the chest into his book bag. He ran home excited about what he found and hid it in a secret hiding place in his backyard.

For days and days, he played with his new treasure.

He built a tall tower with his coins, but the wind blew it down. He dug a hole and buried his treasure like the pirates of old, but his dog dug them up. He went back to the beach and built a sand castle of coins, but the tide washed it away.

He put some coins in his pocket, but he had a hole in his pocket.

Instead of playing with friends, he counted the coins. He didn't tell anyone about his great treasure because he was afraid they would take it away.

After weeks of hiding his treasure, Tommy was so lonely he decided he had to share the secret with his best friend, Wesley. His best buddy couldn't believe his eyes when he saw the chest full of gold coins hidden behind Tommy's clubhouse.

"How much money is in this chest?" Wesley asked, as he sifted coins through his fingers.

Tommy fell back in the grass and stared at clouds floating by. Then he answered with a sigh, "More money than I can ever spend."

"Tommy, you know the old sea captain who lives at the end of the road in the lighthouse?" Wesley asked with excitement in his voice.

"Everybody knows Cap'n Nick," replied Tommy. "He watches the sea to protect Merryville from storms."

"Did you know he hardly has enough money to feed himself? Why don't you share some of your gold coins with him? He could really use the help," said Wesley.

Tommy and Wesley put a few coins in a bag and left them on Cap'n Nick's doorstep with a note that said, "From your friend." They knocked on the door and then hid in the bushes, watching the old sea captain find his gift. Cap'n Nick smiled, looked around and then looked up for a moment before he grabbed his jacket and headed to town.

Watching Cap'n Nick's happiness gave Tommy great joy in his heart. From that day on, Tommy looked for people in Merryville who needed help. He gave sacks of coins to other boys and girls, moms and dads, old folks and poor folks and more.

Tommy never felt lonely again. The smile on his face showed the warmth in his heart.

Are you wondering how long Tommy's treasure lasted? Forever and ever.

For you see, the more love Tommy gave away, the more love he had to give.

JUST THE BEGINNING...

|

Chapter 4

Respecting Others

As I draw the outline of a heart on an old school chalkboard, I pose the following question to an audience of educators: "Today you have the opportunity to fill the empty heart of a child. What will you place in that child's heart?" Through the years, regardless of the faith, socio-economic standing or ethnicity of the audience, there has been agreement that children need these attributes to become all they are meant to be:

Kindness
Compassion
Faith   Love
Loyalty
Generosity
Self-control   Respect   Patience
Courage   Goodness   Humor
Truthfulness   Appreciation
Forgiveness   Joy
Peace

Sadly, the hearts of many of today's children look more like this:

Anger
Disappointment
Restlessness
Sadness
Disrespect   Fear
Ugliness   Tears
Selfishness
Loneliness
Turmoil
Hate
Unforgiveness
Dishonesty
Impatience
Discouragement
Ingratitude

| **59**

There was a time in our society when service to others and respect for property were natural elements of community. Teaching manners and instilling character were cornerstones of public education. Parents looked at the left side of the report card (conduct) before they looked at the right (grades). Kids got in a lot more trouble if they were disrespectful to a teacher than if they made a B-.

As stated in the curriculum introduction, for the last four decades we have emphasized self-esteem rather than self-respect in kids. We have worried more about damaging a child's ego rather than helping him overcome his ego. Consequently, we have far more disrespectful children than respectful children.

When we seek to help kids feel good about themselves (the goal of self-esteem), we teach them to focus on themselves, on how they feel, and on what they want. This perspective keeps children from participating in the world, from striving to learn. It's placing a mirror in their hands so they see only themselves. They can't see others, nor can they see others looking at them. They grow up believing, "It's all about me." This explains the lack of motivation and sense of entitlement plaguing our middle and upper school students.

> **Self-respect is the fruit of discipline, the sense of dignity grows with the ability to say no to oneself.**
>
> -Abraham J. Heschel

When we seek to help kids respect themselves (the goal of self-respect), we teach them to focus on *others,* on how *others* feel, and on what *others* need. This perspective, in turn, leads children to see the world through a window rather than in a mirror. At the window, their image is reflected back to them, but they look through themselves, past themselves, thus growing up believing, "It's more about others and less about me." At the window, their perspective is enlarged. They can see their place in the world. A sense of entitlement is replaced with the desire to achieve a goal.

In the opening lessons, we are beginning the process of changing the viewpoint of your students from the mirror to the window. We're not concerned with magnifying their self-esteem, but rather developing their self-respect. Through this process, your students are learning how to self-regulate their behavior. The intrinsic quality of self-respect translates into motivated, self-disciplined children with a desire to learn and a longing to become all they are meant to be.

Children with self-respect are able to put others ahead of themselves. They feel a responsibility to society because they can see beyond themselves to how their decisions affect those around them. Bullies can't rock their foundation because kids who have self-respect know who they are and what they stand for. They have a balanced view of themselves. Their confidence is balanced with humility, enabling them to develop the noble quality of humble confidence.

Dr. Roy Baumeister, professor of psychology at Florida State University, was a proponent of self-esteem in the early seventies. After decades of research, however; he has since changed his views. Baumeister now recommends the following: "Forget about self-esteem and concentrate more on self-control and self-discipline. Recent work suggests this would be good for the individual and good for society—and might even be able to fulfill some of those promises that self-esteem once made but could not keep."[1]

The result of building self-esteem? Undisciplined, rude, lazy, disrespectful and ill-mannered children who can't learn. The result of helping children develop self-respect? Disciplined, caring, productive, respectful, and well-mannered children who learn their lessons well.

At Manners of the Heart®, we believe every child can develop self-respect and become all they are meant to be. In this week's lesson, your students continue the process of developing self-respect by learning to first respect others.

[1] Baumeister, Roy F., Ph D. Interview. *Florida State University.* N.p., n.d. Web. <http://www.fsu.edu/profiles/baumeister/>.

Big Ideas

- Showing respect, even in the face of disrespect, is always the right thing to do.
- A heart filled with the right stuff will produce respectful words and actions.
- Respectful words and actions reveal the good things in the heart.

Grade-level skills and objectives:

(K) Children begin to develop respect when they learn to stop, look, and listen to others.

(1) You gain the respect of others when you show respect to others.

(2) Showing respect, even in the face of disrespect, is always the right thing to do.

(3) Respecting others grows good seeds in a child's heart.

Stop, Look and Listen

Materials and Preparation

Practice singing "Stop, Look and Listen," so you can teach your students

Wilbur's Words of Wisdom

Show what's in your heart, please;
Use respectful words and deeds!

Guiding Children's Learning

In today's lesson, we begin developing respect in the hearts of your students. To open the lesson, help your children learn "Stop, Look and Listen."

Stop, Look and Listen

Stop what you are doing
It's the only way.

Look 'em in the eye
And show respect today.

Listen with your heart
To hear what others say.

Stop, look and listen
It's the only way.

Attributes
Goodness, Respectfulness

Kindergarten Skills and Objectives:

Children begin to develop respect when they learn to stop, look and listen to others. In this lesson, children will learn the following:
- To stop when someone is talking to them
- To look the other person in the eye
- To listen to what the other person is saying

Ask the children to join you in reciting "Stop, Look and Listen" several times until they can say it without too much hesitation. Then, divide your class into two sections to practice the hand motions. Help them form two rows facing each other so that everyone has a partner. Have each student bow to his partner before beginning the song.

Stop, Look and Listen

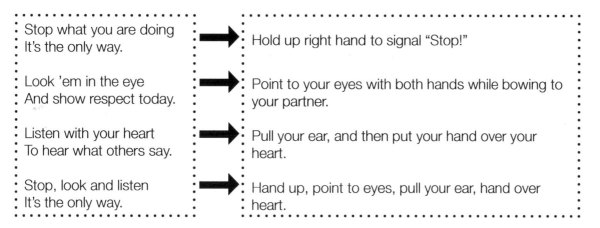

Stop what you are doing It's the only way.	Hold up right hand to signal "Stop!"
Look 'em in the eye And show respect today.	Point to your eyes with both hands while bowing to your partner.
Listen with your heart To hear what others say.	Pull your ear, and then put your hand over your heart.
Stop, look and listen It's the only way.	Hand up, point to eyes, pull your ear, hand over heart.

Have students sing the song to their partner several times using the hand motions.

Continue the lesson by asking your students the following questions:

What did you learn from "Stop, Look and Listen?"
- *To show respect*
- *To bow to others*
- *To stop what I'm doing when someone is talking to me*
- *To look someone in the eye when they're talking to me*
- *To really listen to what someone is saying to me*

What does the word 'respect' mean?
- *To care about others*
- *To treat others well*
- *To obey*
- *To say nice words*
- *To use manners*

Why should you show respect to others?
- *It shows them I care.*
- *It shows them they're special to me.*
- *It shows them I'm trying to do the right thing.*

Do you look adults in the eye when they're talking to you? This shows them respect.

Do you listen really hard to what others are saying to you? This shows them respect.

Where does respect come from? Your head or your heart?
- *It comes from your heart.*
- *It starts in your heart and moves to your head.*
- *It starts in your heart, moves to your head and then comes out in your words and actions.*

What are nice things we can say so others hear the respect in our hearts?

- *I love you.*
- *Please.*
- *Thank you.*
- *Excuse me.*
- *I'm sorry.*
- *Can I help you?*
- *Good morning!*
- *Have a good day!*
- *You go first!*

What are nice things we can do to show the respect in our hearts?

- *Help someone clean up their mess*
- *Hold the door open for others*
- *Smile*

End the lesson by helping students recite "Stop, Look and Listen" again with their partner.

EXTENDING
CHILDREN'S LEARNING

1. Read "A Bully's New Heart" (found at the end of the lesson). Explain how Bully learns to show respect to others when Tommy shows respect to him! You also can help others become respectful by being respectful toward them first. Ask your students the following questions:

   - *Does Bully's heart change in this story?*
   - *What does his heart look like at the beginning?*
   - *What does his heart look like at the end?*
   - *Do Bully's actions and words show what is in his heart? How?*

2. Make a copy of the "Stop for Respect" activity sheet for each student and for your classroom. Let the students color them as they wish. Cut them out and use them as a reminder to show others respect by stopping, looking and listening.

3. Declare this to be "Respect Week." At the beginning of each day this week, ask your students what they will do today to act respectfully in your classroom and around the school. Expect your students to live up to their suggestions and keep them accountable! Here are a few of our ideas:

   - *Say "Please" and "Thank you" with a smile.*
   - *Say "Good morning," "Good afternoon," and "Have a nice day!"*
   - *Offer to open the door for others.*
   - *Let others go first.*
   - *Stop, look and listen when someone wants to speak to you.*

4. Create a class policy to always "Stop, Look and Listen" as a way to respect others when they are speaking! Before group discussions, students could practice the "Stop, Look and Listen" song with hand motions to remember how they should behave while their teacher or classmates are talking. Also, remind students that we listen with our *hearts*, not just by keeping our mouths closed.

Home Connection

Dear Parent/Guardian,

Respect is at the heart of Manners of the Heart®. One of our goals is to help you raise respectful children who become respectable adults. Children begin to develop respect when they learn to stop, look and listen to others. In this week's lesson, your kindergartner is learning the following:

- To stop when someone is talking to them
- To look the other person in the eye
- To listen to what the other person is saying

Here are some ideas to reinforce your child's development of respectful attitudes and actions:

- Try to find wholesome books, television shows and movies that will not only entertain your child, but also teach him or her valuable life lessons. If your child witnesses respectful words and actions, these behaviors will come more naturally.

- Talk with your child about your family's rules concerning television, movies, books, music or magazines. Explain there are some forms of entertainment that don't encourage respectful words or actions and this is why you have these rules.

- If your child has a lot of hurt from his or her past, don't ignore it. Talk to your child and, if needed, seek professional help. It takes a little longer for a child to demonstrate respectful attitudes and actions if his or her heart has experienced too much fear, anger or disappointment.

- If you want your child to respect you, make a point to respect him or her. Have the same expectations for yourself that you have for your child. No one can be perfect, but we can all try to be a little better today than we were yesterday! Live out the qualities you hope to see in your child, and you will inspire your kids to live this way as well. This is a lifelong process. Stay the course with a plan and a purpose to raise a respectful child in spite of our disrespectful world!

~ From Our Hearts To Yours

66 |

Stop for Respect

A BULLY'S
NEW HEART

Tommy woke up from a deep sleep to the rooster's crow one fine morning in Merryville. His first thought was of Bully, his bulldog friend. He remembered how mean Bully had been to PD a few days before. But he felt bad that he had been unkind to Bully when he refused to pet him because he was being so mean to PD.

He thought about how sad Bully's heart must be because he always seemed to be mad about something.

Tommy jumped out of bed and ran downstairs for breakfast. Tommy's mom, Mrs. Tripper, had fixed his favorite bowl of porridge, served up with a tall glass of milk. As he started eating, Tommy said, "Mom, do you remember the two bulldogs I met in town named Buddy and Bully? They looked just alike, except Buddy had a big heart on his chest."

"A big heart on his chest?" asked Mrs. Tripper.

"Well, it really was a white spot that just looked like a heart, but the funny thing is, Buddy really does have a big heart!" answered Tommy. "All Bully does is growl at everybody."

Tommy finished his breakfast and finished his chores, then turned to his mom and asked if he could go to town. "Buddy

asked me to help him show Bully how much more fun it is to not be a bully," Tommy said to his mom.

"Well, honey, I'm sure you can be a big help to Buddy. You've learned how good it is to stand up for what's right," Mrs. Tripper said. "Remember to be home in time for lunch."

Tommy jumped on his bike. He remembered to take it slowly when he got to the top of the hill. He didn't want to end up at the bottom of the big red mailbox again. He shouted, "Morning, Wilbur," as he passed the Happle Tree.

Wilbur replied, "Indeeeed it is. *In* deed!"

Wouldn't you know, Tommy looked ahead to see Buddy and PD, the puppy dog, coming to greet him. "Morning, Tommy," said Buddy.

"Morning, Tommy," said PD. "We are trying to get some of the gang together to play fetch. Will you throw the ball for us?"

"Sure thing, guys," answered Tommy. "Where's Bully? I've been thinking about him this morning."

"I'm sure he'll be along as soon as we start playing," Buddy said with a smirk. So Tommy picked up the ball and threw it. Buddy caught it and brought it back to Tommy. Tommy threw it again, but this time, instead of PD catching it, Bully came from nowhere and nabbed it. Instead of bringing it back to Tommy, he ran down the street as fast as he could, taking the ball with him.

Buddy and Tommy just looked at each other, while PD flopped down on the ground and trembled with his tail tucked between his legs. A tear ran down PD's face as he cried, "Why does Bully always have to be such a bully?"

Tommy jumped on his bike and peddled as fast as he could to catch Bully. As he passed the police station, he saw Bully lying in the grass holding the ball between his paws.

Tommy got off his bike, knelt down, and looked Bully straight in the eye. Then he said, "Bully, what do you think you're doing?"

"I wanted to play, but nobody even asked me," Bully snarled, as he pulled the ball in closer to his chest.

"If you give me the ball, I'll throw it back to you," Tommy said. "And every time you bring it back, I'll throw it to you again."

Tommy kept looking at Bully while he waited for his answer. But Bully was thinking…*Can I trust Tommy? Will he really throw me the ball or will he just take it away?*

Bully looked back at Tommy. Tommy didn't look angry; he looked like he wanted to be friends. So Bully pushed the ball toward Tommy and stood up. Tommy pushed it back to him.
Bully shoved it a little harder toward Tommy. Tommy bounced it back. Bully had to jump to catch it.

Bully thought this could be fun. So he slung

it back to Tommy as he waited with a grin for the next throw. Tommy bounced it back again, and said, "Bully, let's join the others."

Bully caught the ball in mid-air and then stopped in his tracks. "Tommy, can we keep playing, just the two of us?"

Tommy answered, "No, Bully. Buddy and PD are waiting for us. Let's go. You bring the ball."

Bully felt good that Tommy trusted him to bring the ball and not run away with it again.

When they got to the playground, Bully walked right up to PD and dropped the ball in front of him. PD thought it was a trick, but Bully said, "It's your turn, now."

Buddy couldn't believe his own ears. *Did Bully say it was somebody else's turn? Did Bully give PD the ball?*

Tommy reached down to throw the ball for PD. PD raced as fast as he could, knowing he would have to beat Bully to the ball. Much to his surprise, when he caught the ball, he turned around and saw that Bully was just watching and waiting for his turn.

Buddy walked over to Bully and licked him on the side of his face, then put out his paw for a low-five.

They took turns chasing the ball the rest of the morning. Back and forth. Running and jumping with joy. Suddenly, Tommy realized it was lunchtime and that he needed to race home, so he wouldn't be late.

"Guys, I gotta' go," said Tommy. "Can y'all play again tomorrow?"

"Sure thing, Tommy. Same time. Same place," said Bully.

Buddy and Bully told PD to keep the ball,

and then they went home.

That night when Bully was falling asleep, he thought to himself what a fun day he had playing with friends. Instead of going to sleep sad and mad, he went to sleep glad.

His heart felt glad, too!

JUST THE BEGINNING...

Chapter 5

Treating Others

Many years ago, a second-grade student threw his foot into the aisle as I was walking briskly between rows of cafeteria tables. Down I went. Face first. Nose smashed. The foot, of course, belonged to David, the most difficult student I ever had the privilege of teaching. When I looked up, David's electric smile cast shadows across my face, as it had many times before.

No harsh words were spoken.

Believing in my heart that every child can be reached, I had to accept that apparently I would not be the one to reach David. Not one to give up easily, I continued to approach him from behind to touch his shoulder. I wanted David to know I would never give up on him, even though it seemed he had given up on himself.

Fast forward nine years. I was serving lunch on the cafeteria line when a high school junior (who looked more like an NFL tight end) leaned over the counter and said, "Miss Manners, I need to talk to you, please." When I looked up, there was a smile that could light up a Friday night football field. It was David. "I'm really busy right now," I replied with a tremble in my voice as I rubbed the crook in my nose.

"I have something I need to tell you," he insisted. I stepped from behind the line to greet him. With a charming gentleness, he continued, "Miss Manners, I know I gave you a lot of trouble when I was a little kid, but you were always nice to me anyway."

"Oh, you weren't that much trouble, David," I replied.

"When I was a little kid, you were the only one who treated me the way I wanted to be treated...that's what I needed...someone who was nice to me," he finished, leaving me in tears.

Sounds like the Golden Rule turned inside out, doesn't it? David needed someone to treat him the way he wanted to be treated, even though at the time he was incapable of treating others that way.

Fast forward three more years. David graduated with honors and received a scholarship from a prestigious university. But even more impressive, he became one of the finest young men one could ever meet.

Today, David treats others even better than he wants to be treated, evidence he learned the Golden Rule by first experiencing it.

Let's apply the Golden Rule to the opening lessons to see this principle at work:

- Helping others the way you want others to help you.

- Nicholas the pirate became Cap'n Nick the protector when Ol' McDonald helped him, in spite of Nicholas' ingratitude.

- Excusing others the way you want others to excuse you.

  - Sketch and Henry became life-long friends when Henry excused Sketch's thoughtlessness and Sketch, in turn, asked for forgiveness.

- Appreciating others the way you want others to appreciate you.

  - When Tommy shared his treasure with others, he discovered the more he gave away, the more he had to give.

- Respecting others the way you want others to respect you.

  - Bully became a Buddy when Tommy gave him respect, in spite of his disrespectfulness.

- Treating others the way you want to be treated.

  - Albert's self-absorption disappeared when Wilbur helped him learn the Golden Rule. Little did he know that living by the Golden Rule would bring everything he was really hoping for.

We believe hearts are unlocked with love, love expressed in the Golden Rule. When the heart is unlocked, the mind opens to receive knowledge and apply it for the good of society.

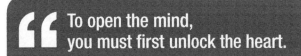

> **To open the mind, you must first unlock the heart.**
>
> -Wise Ol' Wilbur

Children need to experience the love found in the Golden Rule to develop the desire to live by the Golden Rule. We have found that children who learn to love well, learn to live well.

Stacey Bess was a teacher whose accomplishments were so extraordinary that Hallmark told her story in the movie, *Beyond the Blackboard*. She lived by the Golden Rule, treating her students the way she wanted to be treated – with compassion and expectation. She abandoned conventional teaching methods to look beyond the troubles of her students to look inside at the struggles in their hearts. She realized the only way to educate their minds was first to educate their hearts.

Today's society doesn't encourage the Golden Rule. We're told to treat ourselves the way we want others to treat us. Our children are told to love themselves, not others. No wonder there is so much conflict in our schools. We're all loving and 'treating' ourselves, but not each other.

Eleanor Roosevelt once said, "The most important thing in any relationship is not what you get but what you give... the giving of love is an education in itself." Thomas Carlyle, a social commentator in the 1800s, recognized "a loving heart is the beginning of all knowledge."

The Golden Rule and loving others are inseparable. To love is to live by the Golden Rule.

We can practice the Golden Rule by:

- Loving our students enough to treat them the way we want to be treated.
- Loving our students enough to look beyond their troubles on the outside to see the struggles on the inside, just as we hope others would do for us.
- Loving our students enough to give our best, just as we hope to inspire them to give their best in return.
- Loving our students enough to help them learn to help others, appreciate others, respect others and treat others the way they want to be treated.

Loving our students and encouraging them to love others through the Golden Rule begins the education of the heart, the foundation of all education.

Big Ideas

- A child who learns to love well, learns to live well.
- When the heart is unlocked by love, the mind opens to receive knowledge.
- A child who experiences the love found in the Golden Rule develops the desire to live by the Golden Rule.

Grade-level skills and objectives:

(K) Children discover that treating others the way they want to be treated makes the world a better place to live.

(1) The Golden Rule involves giving away the best you have, not keeping it.

(2) The Golden Rule is the foundation of helping, excusing, appreciating, and respecting others.

(3) When you look into someone's heart, you find they have the same needs you do—to love and be loved.

Golden Lessons

Materials and Preparation

- "Albert and the Happle Tree" (found at the end of the lesson)

Wilbur's Words of Wisdom

Treat others the way you want to be treated.

Guiding Children's Learning

Begin today's lesson by reading "Albert and the Happle Tree."

After the story, lead the children in a discussion, using the following questions:

What does the Happle Tree look like?
- *It has a trunk as big around as a merry-go-round.*
- *Its branches stretch across the river and rest on the other side.*
- *The leaves are a hundred shades of green and so thick you can't see the sky.*
- *It's covered in happles.*

What do you learn about Wilbur?
- *He is enormous.*
- *He has a bright yellow beak.*
- *He has eyebrows that curve up to his ears.*
- *He has been around forever and ever.*
- *He has glasses that help him see into hearts.*

What do you learn about Albert McDonald?
- *He was Mrs. McDonald's husband's great, great grandfather.*
- *He had a hound dog named Chester.*
- *He was a boy when he found the Happle Tree.*

What does Albert learn from Wise Ol' Wilbur?
- *The Golden Rule*
- *That happles fill your heart with goodness*
- *You can find the answers you need at the Happle Tree.*

Attributes

Empathy, Humility, Selflessness

Kindergarten Skills and Objectives:

Children discover that treating others the way they want to be treated makes the world a better place to live. In this lesson, children will learn the following:
- To treat others the way they want to be treated
- They can make the world a better place even at their young age!

What is the Golden Rule?
- *Treat others the way you want to be treated.*
- *Help others if you want them to help you.*
- *Share with others if you want them to share with you.*

What does Albert do after he learns the Golden Rule?
- *He offers to help Miss Charlotte make another chocolate Santa Claus.*
- *He gives his friend not one, but two candy bars.*
- *He gives the beggar the rest of his Christmas money.*
- *He helps his pop finish the Christmas sled.*

What happens to Albert on Christmas morning?
- *Miss Charlotte surprises him with a chocolate Santa.*
- *His friend gives him a candy bar.*
- *The sled he helps his pop finish is a special gift for him.*

End the lesson by telling the children to remember the Golden Rule and to use it every day.

Definitions:

EMPATHY
Walking in another person's shoes

HUMILITY
Not caring who gets credit

SELFLESSNESS
Choosing to give of yourself with no expectation of return or consideration of loss

PART 1

EXTENDING
CHILDREN'S LEARNING

1. Have a little fun by teaching your students "Round and Round the Happle Tree," sung to the tune of "Pop Goes the Weasel." In the last line, the children each say their own name.

Round and Round the Happle Tree

Round and round the ha-apple tree
With Wilbur, me and you.
The Golden Rule spreads love all around.
Hey! It's for you!

Round and round the ha-apples go
The home of Wise Ol' Wilbur.
Ol' Wilbur says Who-o-o goes there
Hey! It's _____ (child's name)!

2. Your students can make their very own Happle Tree using "The Happle Tree" and "The Happle Tree Treetop" activity sheets. In addition to the activity sheets, each student will need one sheet of green paper and a glue stick. (Optional—if your students have not mastered cutting or if scissors are limited, you could prepare the happle top cut-outs ahead of time).

   • Fold piece of green paper in half.
   • Place "The Happle Tree Treetop" pattern on the fold and cut out the shape (Your students don't have to be able to follow it exactly!)
   • Open the treetop.
   • Glue in place on The Happle Tree sheet using dotted lines as a guide.
   • Color the trunk of the tree.
   • Students can draw 'happles' (hearts with two leaves) to complete their trees!

3. Throughout the week and for the remainder of the year, remind students about the Golden Rule in the way they treat others. Here are some examples:

   • When you or another student is interrupted, remind the student causing the interruption to treat others the way he wants to be treated. No one likes to be interrupted in the middle of talking, and he should be careful not to interrupt others.
   • Remind the students to include everyone when playing before or after school or during recess. You don't like to be left out, and neither does anyone else!
   • Each time there is a conflict between students, settle it by reminding both students why it is important to treat others the way you want to be treated. Arguments are often caused by one student failing to consider the

PART 1

perspective of another or treating another student unkindly. If everyone treats others the way he wants to be treated, we will all get along!

4. Make a "Wilbur Says…" poster for your classroom using the graphic of Wilbur on the "Wilbur Says" activity sheet. (Also found in the intranet portion of the Manners of the Heart® website, located at www.mannersoftheheart.org under the My Manners tab.) Ask your students to tell you ways they can practice the Golden Rule while you add them to the list. Use this activity to remind students what they learned in the previous lessons. Here are a few ideas:

- Help Others—Offer to carry things for others.
- Excuse Others—Wait, don't whine.
- Appreciate Others—Give compliments often.
- Respect Others—Listen to others.

Finally, here are a few new ideas—
- Keep your things picked up.
- Don't tattle.
- Take turns.
- Share the bathroom.

Home Connection

Dear Parent/Guardian,

"The happle doesn't fall far from the tree." ~ Wise Ol' Wilbur

No, that's not a typo. Your child is learning about happles this week. Wise Ol' Wilbur is the central character of *Manners of the Heart®*. He lives in Merryville in the only Happle Tree in the world. The children of Merryville run to Wilbur for guidance and words of wisdom when they can't find their way. He shares his knowledge through sound advice full of encouragement and practical, everyday solutions. This week, Wilbur is teaching students about the Golden Rule. Kindergartners are learning the following:

- To treat others the way they want to be treated
- That they can make the world a better place even at their young age

Children treat others the way they want to be treated when their heart is filled with love. As your child learns to practice the Golden Rule, here are some of our thoughts on love:

- **Love isn't just an emotion; it's a choice.** You can choose to love when you're angry. You can choose to love when you're disappointed. You can choose to love when you don't feel love.

- **Children love others as they have been loved.** A child whose heart is filled with the love of his parents doesn't need to look in the world for his heart to be filled. Time, discipline, and words of affirmation fill a child's heart.
    - Time spent just being together… listening, talking, working on projects.
    - Loving enough to discipline. Children who are not disciplined grow up resenting their parents who didn't train them to be responsible.
    - Children who are demeaned with words that attack their *being*, rather than their behavior, develop bitterness and rebellion.

- **Here are a few fun ways to "go the extra mile" in showing love this week:**
    - Serve heart-shaped pancakes for breakfast.
    - Fill the book bag, purse or briefcase of your family members with love notes.
    - Prepare a special supper of everyone's favorite foods.
    - Leave the television off for the evening and enjoy each other's company.
    - Read a chapter-a-night from an old classic before bedtime with the whole family.
    - Give out real hugs and kisses and say "I love you" as you tuck everyone in for the night.

~ From Our Hearts To Yours

78 |

The Happle Tree

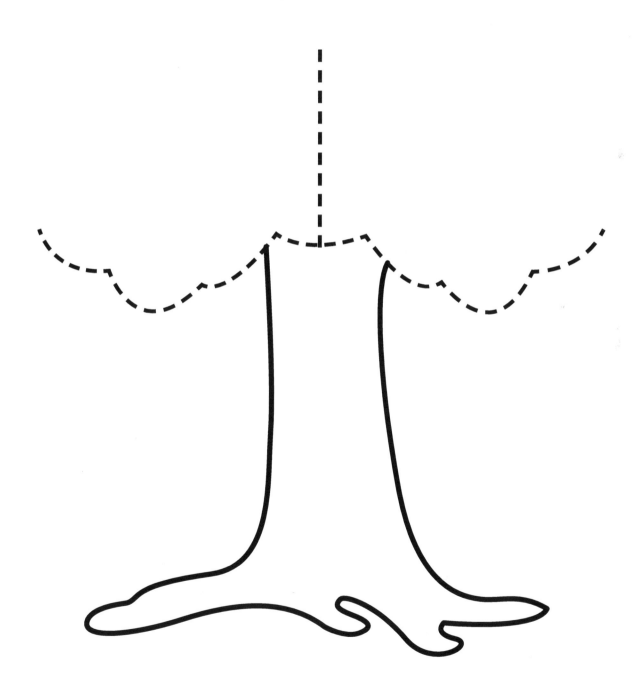

| **79**

PART 1

The Happle Tree Treetop

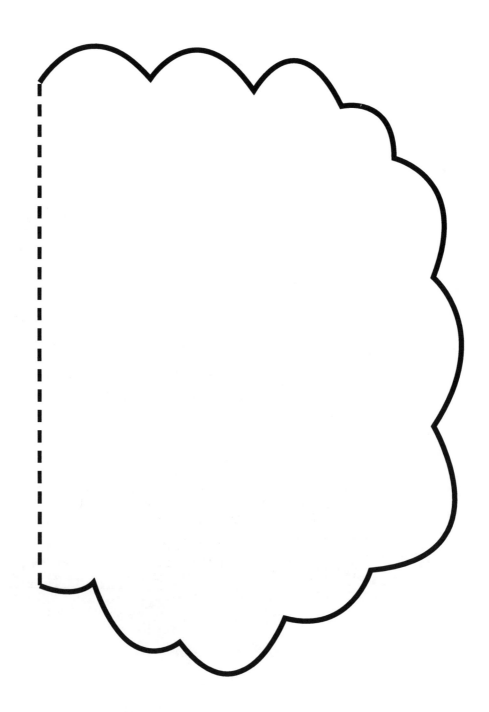

|

Wilbur Says

ALBERT AND
THE HAPPLE TREE

Tommy and his friends had been fishing all day. Before they headed home, they decided to stop by Mrs. McDonald's house to say hello. Wouldn't you know it? She was just taking chocolate chip cookies out of the oven. Before they could ask, she invited them in for a snack.

Tommy took one bite of those cookies and said, "Mrs. McDonald, these really are the best chocolate chip cookies I've ever tasted."

"Glad you like 'em, Tommy. It's an old family recipe," replied Mrs. McDonald.

"How old?" quizzed Tommy.

"Well, so old, I don't know how old," answered Mrs. McDonald with a chuckle.

"Sounds like the Happle Tree. Nobody knows how old it is either," said Tommy.

"That's right, but did you know my great-great-grandfather, Albert McDonald, discovered the Happle Tree when he was just a boy?" answered Mrs. McDonald.

"Will you tell us the story?" Tommy asked.

"I'd be happy to, Tommy. It's my favorite story to tell…
It was a cold wintry morning in Merryville.

Snow had been falling for days on end. Christmas was only a week away. Little Albert's pop was working in his workshop, trying to finish a sled for a special Christmas gift. His pop had spent long hours building it. Albert often wondered who would receive the sled.

"Albert, time is running out. The runners still need to be painted. Would you do that today?" Albert's pop asked.

Albert thought, *Why should I paint runners for someone else's sled?*

"Pop, I don't have time today. I have to go to town," answered Albert.

"But, Albert, I really need your help," said Albert's pop.

"Don't have time now, pop," Albert said, as he ran out of the workshop.

Chester, Albert's faithful hound dog, came running from the barn to join him. Chester followed Albert all the way to town. Once they made it to town, Albert and Chester passed an old man who was asking for money to help his family at Christmas. Albert slowed down, but instead of dropping money into the beggar's cup, he ran into Miss Charlotte's

Chocolate Shop to buy his favorite twenty-

|

five cent candy.

One of Albert's buddies came up to him in the chocolate shop and asked for a piece of his candy. Albert said, "Not today."

"But, Albert," said his friend, "I gave you some of my candy last week."

"But you had a lot more candy than I do," Albert replied, and headed toward the door with two bars in his hand.

Running out of the chocolate shop, he bumped a table and knocked a chocolate Santa Claus to the floor. Miss Charlotte was talking to a customer and didn't see what happened. Albert kept going without picking up the broken Santa Claus.

"Let's go, Chester," Albert said. The two headed for their favorite walk in the woods.

Albert picked up a stick and threw it for Chester to fetch. While he was waiting for Chester to bring it back, he unwrapped his candy bar and took a big bite. Chester brought the stick back. Albert threw it again, but this time he decided to run after Chester. Not looking where he was going, he tripped over something under the snow and fell to the ground. Chester jumped to

help him. "Chester, I'm all right, boy. See if you can find out what's under there," said Albert as he pulled himself up from the snow.

Chester started digging in the snow, sniffing and pawing as he went. It didn't take long to find out what had tripped his master. Chester barked, as he pointed to the root of a giant tree that had been hidden under days of snow.

Albert helped Chester clear the snow and trace the root of the great tree back to its trunk. "This thing is huge, Chester. It must be big around as a merry-go-round. What do you think?" asked Albert. Chester circled the tree and barked in agreement.

The snow was barely falling now as Albert looked up to see the most amazing tree he had ever laid his eyes on. As he stared in disbelief, his mouth dropped open. Chester's mouth dropped open, too.

Towering over them stood a tree like no other. The leaves were a hundred shades of green and so thick they could hardly see the sky. The tree's branches reached to the clouds and stretched across the river to rest on the other side. Hanging from the branches were bright red balls that looked kind of like hearts.

Suddenly, they heard a call from the highest part of the tree, "Whooooo goes there?"

Before they could answer, snow from the branches of the tree covered their faces. From inside the tree, an enormous owl swooped down to sit on the big branch in front of them. He was speckled grey with giant eyebrows that curved to his ears. His bright yellow beak looked like it had been painted. The owl spoke again, "I said, whooooo goes there?"

Surprised, but not scared, Albert answered, "I'm Albert McDonald, and this here dog is

PART 1

Chester."

To which the owl replied, "Nice to meet you, Albert and Chester. I'm Wise Ol' Wilbur. Folks say I know a lot about a lot of things," Wilbur answered.

"Well, then, sir, can you tell me about this fine tree you're sittin' in? I've never seen a tree the likes of this one," replied Albert.

Wilbur snickered, "That's because there's no other tree like it. This is the world's only Happle Tree."

"Happle Tree? What's a happle?" Albert asked.

"Happles are the fruit of my tree," he continued.

"Your tree? Did you say this is your tree?" Albert jumped in.

"I did. I've lived in this tree for a looong, looong time," answered Wilbur.

"How long is that?" asked Albert.

"Forever and ever," said Wilbur as he reached up and plucked a happle from his tree. "Now, to answer your first question…A happle is a fruit filled with goodness that's shaped like a heart and tastes sweet as an apple. That's why they're called happles."

"They sure do look good to eat," said Albert.

"They are good to eat, Albert, but they're not just good for your belly, they're good for your heart, too," said Wilbur, putting on his glasses to look into Albert's heart.

"Whooooo, I see trouble in there. Trouble, indeed," said Wilbur.

"Wilbur, what do you mean, trouble in

there?" asked Albert.

"Well, Albert," answered Wilbur. "When I put on my glasses, I can see into little boys' and little girls' hearts."

"What do you see in my heart, Wilbur?" asked Albert.

"I see a heart that needs to learn the Golden Rule. A heart that needs to learn how to treat others the way you want to be treated," answered Wilbur.

"What do you mean?" asked Albert. "I see a broken chocolate Santa in Miss Charlotte's shop because you didn't stop to pick it up or apologize," said Wilbur.

"But I was in a hurry," answered Albert.

"Wouldn't you want someone to apologize if they broke something of yours?" asked Wilbur.

"I see you didn't share your candy with a friend who shared his candy with you last week," said Wilbur.

"But he had more than I did," answered Albert.

"I see an old beggar man who needed help, but you didn't help him," said Wilbur.

"But I needed my money to buy my favorite candy bars," answered Albert.

"I see your father asking you for help building a sled, but you didn't have time," said Wilbur. "Don't you want your father's help when you need help?" Albert felt bad, but didn't know what to do.

"Albert, I suggest you try a happle for your heart," said Wilbur as he plucked a happle, polished it on his chest, and handed it to Albert. "A happle a day keeps the trouble away," added Wilbur.

Albert took a bite of the happle and said, "Mmmmmm, that *is* good. Let's go, Chester, we have a lot of work to do."

On the way back to town, Albert decided he would apologize to Miss Charlotte and offer to help her make another chocolate Santa. And he decided to give his friend a bar of chocolate. But then thought, *No, I'll give him two.* And he decided the old beggar man needed the rest of his money.

When he returned home, his pop was not quite finished with the sled. Albert asked if there was anything he could do. His pop said, "Why don't you tighten the screws and polish the runners?" So Albert finished the work on the sled, turned out the workshop lights, and headed for bed.

Albert drifted off to sleep thinking of the things he had learned that day. *I have learned to apologize, to share, and to help others when they need it. Now I know how to treat others the way I want to be treated.*

"Boy, that was a great story," said Tommy. "Sounds like your great-great-grandfather learned a lot from Wilbur."
"He sure did," answered Mrs. McDonald. "Albert never forgot the Christmas he learned the Golden Rule. On Christmas morning, Miss Charlotte surprised him with a chocolate Santa. His friend came by with a chocolate bar, and the sled he helped his pop finish was a gift for Albert. In fact, the sled you use when you speed down Merryville Mountain is Albert's sled!"

Mrs. McDonald looked at the old sled leaning against the wall by the door…just waiting to be used.

JUST THE BEGINNING…

| **85**

Part 2   Everyday Courtesies

Chapter  6

Becoming Ladies and Gentlemen

This is the lesson that brings out my deep Southern heritage. Nothing was more important to my mother than raising four ladies and a gentleman. We weren't wealthy city folks. We were country bumpkins living on a dead end road several miles out from town.

We were expected to say, "Yes, Ma'am" and "Yes, Sir" to adults as the beginning of understanding respect for authority. We were taught to give up our seats for the elderly and to never, under any circumstances, say an unkind word about anyone. We were encouraged to look for ways to make someone else's day a little better. Mother always said, "You find your happiness by making someone else happy."

When mother pulled my hair into a tight ponytail before school in the mornings, she would always remind me that "Pretty is as pretty does." She taught me how to sit like a lady, walk like a lady, and talk like a lady. But as a little squirt with over-sized buck teeth, I had my share of bullying by mean girls. Mother said, "If you do the right thing because it's the right thing to do, it doesn't matter what anyone else thinks or does. Sooner or later, they'll leave you alone when they find out they can't tear you down. Right is right." She was right.

This lesson will help you teach a young girl to appreciate how special it is to be a lady. She'll learn how to behave like a lady, talk like a lady, and be respected as a lady. Your girls will learn that by allowing boys to treat them as ladies should be treated, they will develop self-respect within their own hearts.

Teaching young boys how to treat girls and ladies with respect enables them to restrain from inappropriate behavior as they grow up. Well-developed manners become the foundation for morals in the teen years.

Teaching young boys how to become gentlemen and teaching young girls how to become ladies is one of the greatest lessons children can be taught. You'll be amazed how your students will embrace these objectives.

Kindergartners learn how to let others go first. Looking for ways to be helpful enables first-graders to practice being ladies and gentlemen. The hearts of second-graders become sensitive to the feelings of others. Making a commitment to honor others above themselves, third-graders begin to internalize the attributes of graciousness and gentleness.

We hope you will enjoy teaching your students how to become ladies and gentlemen. We'll all reap the benefits.

| **87**

PART 2

PART 2

Big Ideas

- Girls begin to learn that by allowing boys to treat them as a lady should be treated, they develop self-respect within their own hearts.
- Boys begin to understand that showing respect for others, especially young ladies, is an important part of becoming a well-mannered young man filled with self-respect.
- A boy with a kind heart becomes a man with a good heart.
- A girl who respects others becomes a lady who respects herself.
- Well-developed manners in young children become the foundation for morals in the teen years.

Grade-level skills and objectives:

(K) Children begin to understand how to be gentlemen and ladies by letting others go first and by politely accepting the invitation to go first.

(1) Children show an awareness of gracious and gentle behavior towards others by looking for ways to be helpful.

(2) Showing concern for the feelings of others comes straight from the hearts of ladies and gentlemen.

(3) Striving to become a lady or a gentleman requires a commitment to honor others above one's self.

|

You Go First

Materials and Preparation

- None

Wilbur's Words of Wisdom

A lady waits and says, "Thank you."
A gentleman says, "After you."

"After You" Song for Boys:
   After you, then I'll go through,
   I'll go through, I'll go through.
   After you, then I'll go through,
   My fair lady.

"Thank You Kindly, Sir" Song for Girls:
   Thank you very kindly sir,
   Kindly sir, kindly sir.
   Thank you very kindly, sir,
   My thanks to you.

Guiding Children's Learning

Begin the lesson by asking the children to tell about a time when someone else allowed them to go first and then to tell about a time when they let someone else go first.

Explain to the children that when they put someone else first, they are behaving like ladies and gentlemen. Ask the following questions:

Can a little girl or boy behave like a lady or gentleman? How?

What kinds of things might they do?
- *Use inside voices.*
- *Boys can let girls go first.*
- *Girls can let other girls or older people go first.*
- *Girls can say "Thank you" when a boy lets them go first.*
- *Be nice to others.*

Attributes
Gentleness, Graciousness

Kindergarten Skills and Objectives:

Children will show courtesy by treating others with the respect due their gender and their age. They will demonstrate an understanding of self-respect, graciousness and gentleness when interacting with others.
- Children will learn that ladies and gentlemen use inside voices.
- Boys will learn to allow girls and elders to go first.
- Girls will wait for the offer to go first, and then politely thank the gentleman.

PART 2

Introduce a movement activity, "After You." Follow these steps:

1. Have the children form two groups—a group of boys and a group of girls.

2. Choose one child from each group to form a doorway by clasping their hands and raising their arms similar to what is done in the children's game, "London Bridge."

3. Have the other two groups each form a line facing the "open door."

4. Sing the following verse to the tune of "London Bridge":

    Welcome, friends; and please, come in.
    Please, come in; please, come in.
    Welcome, friends; and please, come in.
    Come in today.

5. Have the boys take turns standing to the side and motioning to a girl to go first as they sing:

    After you, then I'll go through,
    I'll go through, I'll go through.
    After you, then I'll go through,
    My fair lady.

6. Girls will respond by waiting and then singing:

    Thank you very kindly, sir,
    Kindly sir, kindly sir.
    Thank you very kindly, sir,
    My thanks to you.

Remind the students that ladies and gentlemen always use "inside voices," so have them whisper or sing the song softly to remember. Repeat the activity, allowing children to take turns being the "door."

Conclude the lesson by reviewing the following ideas:

*   A gentleman always allows ladies, young or old, to go first.
*   A lady should wait for a gentleman to allow her to go first, and then thank him.
*   Ladies and gentlemen always use inside voices.
*   If time allows, choose one or more activities from **Extending Children's Learning.**

Definitions:

GENTLENESS
Speaking and acting with tenderness

GRACIOUSNESS
Being courteous, understanding and generous in all situations

EXTENDING
CHILDREN'S LEARNING

1. Have children draw their faces on cardstock circles and then attach them to a craft stick. Describe different actions used by ladies and gentlemen and have students indicate whether they perform them by raising their face. Some examples include the following:

   - I let a girl go ahead when I am getting in line.
   - I let my mom go first when we go through the door at home.
   - I let my teacher go first when entering the classroom.
   - I let my grandma go first when we get in the car.
   - I say "Thank you" when a boy or another girl lets me go first.

2. On your classroom board, draw two columns. Label one with a smiling face and the other with a frowning face. Give examples of situations in which boys or girls put others first or put themselves first. After each, have the children tell you whether the behavior was gentle and kind (smiling face) or unkind (frowning face) while you put a mark in the column. Here are some ideas:

   - I let the girl behind me go first on the slide.
   - I made sure to get to the door first.
   - I ran to be first in the drinking line.
   - I let my teacher go through the door first.
   - I let a friend go first in the snack line.

3. Play the game "Odd Man Out" using your own scenarios or the ones listed above. To play, have three students stand before the class. One of your students will be the "odd man" who is not acting like a lady or a gentleman. Describe a pretend situation for each student, in which each student is/is not acting like a lady or a gentleman. Ask the remaining students to identify the "odd man." Whoever correctly identifies the "odd man" replaces him in the game using a different scenario.

4. Have children role-play scenarios illustrating ways to put others first. Use the ideas and situations discussed earlier in the week so students can practice being ladies and gentlemen. Throughout the week, remind them of how ladies and gentlemen should act while they are playing or participating in discussion.

3. Read the Merryville story "Rescue at the Fall Fair." Afterwards, lead a discussion on how ladies and gentlemen care for the feelings of others.

PART 2

Home Connection

Dear Parent/Guardian,

In this week's lesson, kindergartners are learning how to behave like ladies and gentlemen. Through games and role-play activities, they are learning that gentlemen put ladies—both young and old—first, and that ladies are appreciative of the respect they are shown by politely saying "Thank you" and also by letting other girls and elders go first. Children are playing a game using the following songs sung to the tune of "London Bridge":

"After You" Song for Boys:

> After you, then I'll go through,
> I'll go through, I'll go through.
> After you, then I'll go through,
> My fair lady.

"Thank You Kindly, Sir" Song for Girls:

> Thank you very kindly, sir,
> Kindly sir, kindly sir.
> Thank you very kindly, sir,
> My thanks to you.

Ask your child to tell you if they consider themselves to be a lady or a gentleman and why. Give examples of times you have acted like a lady or a gentleman. Look for moments to let your child see your gentleness and graciousness in action! Gentle reminders of putting others first will help reinforce the common courtesy being learned and practiced this week.

Thank you for your partnership in achieving the goal of good manners!

~ From Our Hearts To Yours

RESCUE AT
THE FALL FAIR

One of the most treasured events of the year in Merryville has always been the annual Fall Fair at the elementary school. Mothers and dads, grandparents, aunts and uncles all come to the school for good old-fashioned fun and good music.

Each year a different grade is given the honor of serving as hosts and hostesses of the fair. This year, it is none other than the second-graders! They have three main duties: to greet everyone as they enter the fairgrounds, to give directions to the games, and to hand out programs for the special show at the end of the day.

The second-graders are really excited because they will also carry on a tradition that has lasted more than one hundred years in Merryville—the singing of "The Star-Spangled Banner" to close the show. The children have been working for weeks and weeks perfecting the song. They've practiced their lines and even memorized the words.

The big day was finally here.

Everyone was having a good time. Wesley won the watermelon-eating contest for the second year in a row. Trey won the softball throw when his ball was the only ball to go through a tiny hoop. The dunking booth had the longest line because everyone wanted to see Mr. Watson, the school's principal, land in the water! He was a favorite because he always came up laughing!

Right in the middle of all the fun, the schoolyard bell rang, signaling the big show was about to begin. Mr. Watson left his perch in the dunking booth and dried off. Miss Charlotte covered her table of chocolate goodies with a cloth to protect them from Carolina, Mrs. McDonald's yard cow who loves milk chocolate.

The children ran backstage in the auditorium to get ready for the show, while the adults were finding their seats. Brianna and Jasmine huddled together with Mary, Allie, and Caroline to go through the words of the closing song one more time.

When all the children were ready, Miss Carter, the music director, led them outside the auditorium to line up at the front door. Sketch, the skunk, and Henry, the turtle, greeted the children as they rushed in to find their seats. PD, Buddy, KC, and Bully gathered around the windows to watch the big show.

Mr. Watson welcomed everyone. The drums rolled, and the cymbals clashed as the doors opened for the kids to march down the aisles to the stage. Everyone in the room jumped to their feet and cheered.

The show had begun!

The kindergartners took turns acting out their favorite nursery rhymes. The first-graders shared artwork and poems they had written. Each of the third-graders played a different musical instrument, including a xylophone, a triangle, a wooden block, a harmonica, hand-bells and even a keyboard.
It was a great show!

When the time came for the grand finale, the second-graders took center stage. The kids lined up with their black top hats and red bowties. Brianna stepped forward to sing the first lines of "The Star-Spangled Banner" all by herself.

Miss Carter played a note on the piano to set the pitch for Brianna.

Brianna took a deep breath and started singing,

"O beautiful for spacious skies…"

But that was the opening line to the wrong song! A few people gasped as everyone realized she was singing the wrong words. A few people even started laughing. Brianna didn't know what to do. She was so embarrassed that she just stopped. Tears ran down her face.

Just as she turned to run off the stage, Mary stopped her and picked up right where she left off,

"…for amber ways of grain."

Jasmine and Allie chimed in.

"For purple mountains majesty, above the fruited plains."

Terrell, Trey, Wesley, and Tommy joined Caroline as she raised her hands for everyone in the audience to join in,

"America, America, God shed his grace on thee."

The laughter stopped, and everyone began singing. When it was over, Brianna hugged her friends and thanked them for rescuing her. They all turned to the flag and placed their hands over their hearts. This time when Miss Carter gave the pitch, together they sang,

"O, say can you see by the dawn's early light…"

As the students carefully sang each heartfelt line of the song, the audience began to join in. One by one, they stood and placed their own hands on their hearts until together, they belted out the last line:

"O'er the land of the free and the home of the brave."

Another ending to a great Merryville Fall Fair!

JUST THE BEGINNING…

Chapter 7

Being a Host

We like to make it an "experience" to visit the Manners of the Heart® office. Behind our red front door, seven-foot Wilbur greets our guests. Brightly colored rooms filled with artwork created by our esteemed kindergartners make a visit to Manners of the Heart® unforgettable. However; we realize that much more important than our office *environment* is our office *hospitality*.

What is most significant when someone visits your home, classroom, or office is not how impressed they were by the surroundings, but rather how they felt after spending time there. Did they feel welcomed and cared for? Were they treated with sincere kindness? Do they want to return?

Late author and educator Henrietta Mears once said, "Hospitality should have no other nature than love." In other words, to be 'given to hospitality' is simply to be 'giving of love.' To take this idea one step further, a good host makes his or her guest *feel loved*.

As an educator, you possess incredible influence over your students' developing social abilities. Each time someone enters your room, impressionable minds and hearts are carefully watching your interactions with your guest. Your students notice whether you treat each individual the same, with patience and kindness or with shortness and irritation. No matter how seemingly insignificant, each interaction teaches a nearby child a life lesson on hospitality.

At Manners of the Heart®, we believe teaching children hospitality involves their learning *generosity*. We all appreciate generosity in others, but it takes time to develop in ourselves. In these lessons, children will learn the foundation of becoming good hosts. We start in kindergarten with the basics of politely saying "hello" and "goodbye" to guests. First-graders learn how to be generous hosts to guests at their own birthday parties. In second grade, students learn how to consider the needs of their guests during snack or mealtime. And finally, third-graders are taught to exercise hospitality overnight as the days of "sleepovers" begin.

> **Manners are a sensitive awareness of the feelings of others. If you have that awareness, you have good manners, no matter what fork you use.**
>
> -Emily Post

| **95**

PART 2

Big Ideas

- Being a good host shows your guest that you care about him or her.
- A good host is a generous host.
- A good host makes his or her guest feel welcome.
- Ladies and gentlemen are good hosts to their guests.

Grade-level skills and objectives:

K Children learn that hospitality begins with welcoming your guests into the home and ends with saying "thank you" for coming.

1 A good host shows generosity to their guests, even when he or she is the birthday boy/girl.

2 A good host not only knows how to politely say "hello" and "goodbye," but also helps his/her guest feel welcome during snack or mealtime.

3 Students learn how to exercise hospitality and generosity towards their guest while hosting a sleepover.

96 |

Thank You For Coming!

Materials and Preparation

- Peter puppet
- "Peter is Hosting" script (Become familiar with the script.)

Wilbur's Words of Wisdom

When you're the host,
Walk to the door
To say "Hi" and "Bye,
Please, come more."

Guiding Children's Learning

Remind students of last week's lesson, in which they learned that gentlemen let ladies go first and that ladies politely say "Thank you" when they are invited to go first. Ask them if they have practiced being ladies and gentlemen this week and let them share some examples.

Explain that now you will talk about what it means to be a lady or a gentleman when you have someone in your home. Use the following questions and comments as a guide:

What does it mean to be a "host"?
- *To have a friend or a family member visit in your house*
- *To play with a friend at your house*

What does it mean to be a guest?
- *To visit in someone else's home*
- *A friend or relative who visits your home is your guest.*

What does it mean to be a good host?
- *To be nice to your guest*
- *To make sure your guest has a good time in your home*
- *To be a lady or a gentleman to your guest*
- *A good host helps a guest feel happy!*

Attributes

Generosity, Hospitality

Kindergarten Skills and Objectives:

Good hospitality begins with welcoming your guests into the home and ends with saying "Thank you" for coming. In this lesson, students will learn the following:
- To greet and welcome their guest(s) at arrival
- To let their guest(s) know they are happy to have them there
- To walk guest(s) to the door when leaving

PART 2

Being a good host does not have anything to do with what your house looks like!

Why is it important to be a **good** host?
- *Helps your friend or family member have a good time and want to return*
- *Shows your guest that you are happy he/she came to your home*
- *Shows your guest that you care about him/her*

Use the following script and Peter puppet to help the children understand how to be a good host:

"Peter is Hosting"

Teacher:	Boys and girls, Peter is here today because he wants to make sure he will be a good host.
Peter:	That's right! I invited Tommy over to my house. I want to make sure he knows I am really happy he is coming over and I will treat him well.
Teacher:	Absolutely, Peter, we will be happy to help you! Boys and girls, what do you think Peter should do when Tommy rings the doorbell? (Wait for responses. If they need coaching, remind them that they need to answer the door.)
Peter:	Oh, yes! Once he rings the doorbell, I will go answer the door so I don't keep him waiting. What should I say when I open the door?
Teacher:	Hmmmm, what do you guys think he should say? (Wait for response. If needed, remind them to say "hello.")
Peter:	Of course! I will say hello and "Welcome to my home!" so he feels comfortable. I want to make sure he knows how happy I am that he is coming over.
Teacher:	That will make Tommy feel very welcome Peter. What do you think you should do if Tommy is carrying something or has a backpack or coat on? (Wait for response. If needed, explain that he should help him with his belongings by hanging up his coat or setting down his bag.)
Peter:	That's right! It would not be nice to make him wear his coat around all day, and he would not know where to put it!
Teacher:	Do you know what to do when it is time for him to go home?
Peter:	I think so, but I am confused… Should I just say goodbye?
Teacher:	Well, what do you think? (Wait for response.) You should walk him to the front door, Peter. It's called showing your guest out. This shows that you

Peter: are a good host.
Okay, that makes sense! I don't want him to feel like he has to walk around by himself. It is polite for me to stop what I am doing and walk him to the door.

Teacher: Exactly, Peter! What do you think you should say to your guest when you show Tommy out? (Wait for children's responses.)

Peter: Well… I think I should tell him "Thank you for coming," and I probably should tell him knows I had a good time.

> ### Definitions:
>
> **GENEROSITY**
> Gladly and willingly giving your time, your talent and your treasure
>
> **HOSPITALITY**
> Serving others with the purpose of making them feel cared for and comfortable

that I enjoyed his visit so he

Teacher: That's right! You've learned a lot. Do you feel like you know what to do now?

Peter: Yes, I do! I would not have been able to do it without you! Thanks, everybody!

Teacher: No problem! Have a fun time with Tommy!

After the role-play, make sure to review with the class the necessary things a good host should do when having a friend over. Don't forget these key points:

- Stop what you are doing and say "Hello" to your guest when he or she arrives.
- Say, "Welcome to my home!"
- Help him/her with belongings.
- See your guest to the door when he or she is leaving.
- Tell your guest, "Thank you for coming! I enjoyed your visit!"

Close by allowing the students to take turns practicing being the host. Have each child greet their guest by saying, "Hello! Welcome to my home/classroom!" and then show their guest out by walking the guest to the door of your classroom and saying, "Thank you for coming! I enjoyed your visit."

PART 2

| **99**

EXTENDING
CHILDREN'S LEARNING

1. Use construction paper and yarn to have students create their own "Welcome" sign to hang on the door of their home or bedroom. Help the children write "Welcome" on the front of their sign (If class time is limited, you can do this beforehand.) and give them coloring utensils to draw pictures on their sign. Then, give each student some string or yarn and help them punch a hole in the top two corners for the string to go through. Help the students tie the string onto their finished sign. Remind them to hang their sign in a place where any guests will see it and feel welcomed. If you like, students can pick a sign to hang on the door of your classroom so guests will feel welcomed into your room.

2. With your students, decide on a class policy for what to do and say when a visitor comes to your classroom. Here are some ideas:

    *   Decide on a special word or phrase to say to your guest as a class. (e.g., "Greetings!" or "Welcome to our class!")
    *   Decide on a special word or phrase to say as your guest is leaving. (e.g., "Thank you for coming! Have a nice day!")
    *   Create a plan for who will greet your guest at the door and who will see your guest out when leaving.

3. Give your students more opportunities to practice their new policy on hosting by arranging to have classroom visitors stop by randomly throughout the week. Assign different students to play the role of "host" by welcoming your guest(s) into the classroom and seeing your guest(s) to the door.

4. Make a note card that says "Hello" and one that says "Goodbye." Hold each one up and have the students tell you different, friendly ways to say "Hello" (i.e. "Greetings!", "Good morning!", "Good afternoon!", "Hola!") and "Goodbye" (i.e. "See you later!", "Farewell!", "Thanks for coming!", "Adios!") to a guest.

5. Throughout the week, pick two students at random to role-play. One can be a guest and the other a host. Make sure to discuss afterwards in order to reinforce the lesson. (Tell the students they will have another opportunity to practice this after learning how to "Be a Guest" in the next lesson.) Students may also use the puppets to practice.

Home Connection

Dear Parent/Guardian,

This week, children are learning what it means to be a good host. Kindergartners are practicing being a good host by greeting their guest when he/she arrives and by showing their guest to the door when he or she leaves. Children are learning that being a good host is one great way to show they are a lady or a gentleman.

Providing even young children with opportunities to practice being a good host helps them internalize these objectives in order to exercise hospitality as adults. This week, create an opportunity for your child to have a friend or a relative over. (Remember, it does not matter to a child where you live or how messy you might think your house is!) Before the visitor arrives, discuss with your child different ways to be a good host to his or her guest. Here are a few key objectives your kindergartner is learning this week:

- Stop what you are doing and say "Hello" to your guest when he or she arrives.
- Say "Welcome to my home!"
- Help him/her with belongings.
- See your guest to the door when he or she is leaving.
- Tell your guest, "Thank you for coming! I enjoyed your visit."

~ From Our Hearts To Yours

MANNERS *of the* **HEART**®

Being a Guest

When my twin sons were seven years old, we attempted to have one of their classmates over on a Saturday afternoon after their soccer game. Mike (name changed to protect the guilty) complained that fishing in the nearby pond was 'boring.' The picnic lunch was 'stupid,' and making homemade chocolate chip cookies with extra chocolate squares on top was 'for girls.' All of these activities happened to be favorite pastimes of my sons and many of their friends who came to visit. But not Mike. He was miserable and made the rest of us miserable, too.

The last straw came when I put supper in front of Mike, and he proclaimed, "I don't want chicken. I want to go to McDonald's." I don't have anything against McDonald's, but when a child is a guest in my home, he will eat what I offer—or go hungry!

Now, it really wasn't eight-year-old Mike's fault he was so rude. No one had taught him how to appreciate being a guest in someone's home. No one had taught him how to be polite when someone was trying to be nice to him.

The saddest part of the story isn't that the boys and I were miserable. The boys could always invite other friends over and enjoy doing the same things Mike hated doing. The saddest part of the story is that Mike could never have a good time anywhere he went.

Just as you had the opportunity to *show* your students how to be good hosts, you can help them learn to be good guests, too. Encourage your children to remember The Golden Rule—treat others the way you want to be treated. Asking the most important question of all, "How would you feel if someone treated you this way?" really does help a child understand how hurtful his actions can be.

In this week's lesson, kindergartners will learn that guests politely greet their host(s) upon arrival and express their appreciation when leaving. First-graders will understand that being a guest at a birthday party is about making the birthday child feel special. In second-grade, children are taught that it's important for guests to be polite during meal times, always making sure to be thankful for the food and invitation. The third-graders will gain an appreciation for the opportunity of a sleepover.

When children understand how much more fun they have when they're polite and appreciative, they'll make the right decisions themselves about being good guests.

102 |

Big Ideas

- Appreciating the hospitality of your host is the beginning of being a good guest.
- Practicing The Golden Rule when you're a guest helps everyone have a good time!
- Polite behavior shows the appreciation in your heart for the privilege of visiting in someone's home.

Grade-level skills and objectives:

(K) Guests politely greet their hosts upon arrival and express their appreciation when leaving.

(1) At a birthday party, good guests remember that the party is for their friend and make sure their friend has a good time.

(2) Guests are polite during meal times, always making sure to be thankful for the food and for the invitation.

(3) Overnight guests are polite to show their appreciation for the opportunity to spend the night in a friend's home.

PART 2

| **103**

You Say Hello and I Say Good-bye

Materials and Preparation

- Peter puppet
- "Peter the Polite Guest" Script (Become familiar with the script.)

Wilbur's Words of Wisdom

A good guest knows to be polite
And say "Thank you" to share delight!

Guiding Children's Learning

Remind the students what they have already learned about being ladies and gentlemen and about being a good host. Ask them to tell you what it means to be a host:

- *To have a friend or a family member over to your house*
- *To play with a friend at your house*

Ask them to remind you what it means to be a **good** host?

- *To be nice to your guest*
- *To make sure your guest has a good time in your home*
- *To be a lady or a gentleman to your guest*
- *A good host helps a guest feel happy!*

Now, explain that since they already know how to be a good host, today they will learn how to be a good guest. Use the following questions and comments to guide the students:

What does it mean to be a guest?

- *To visit in someone else's home*
- *You are the guest when you visit a friend or family member's home.*
- *To join a friend on an outing (e.g. to the museum, to the zoo, to a restaurant, etc.)*

Attributes

Appreciation, Politeness

Kindergarten Skills and Objectives:

Guests politely greet their hosts upon arrival and express their appreciation when they are leaving. In this lesson, children will learn the following:

- To knock or ring the doorbell to a friend's home before entering
- To say hello to their friend and any others in the home (their friend's parents, siblings, etc.)
- To express their appreciation when they are leaving by saying "Goodbye. Thank you for having me," or "I enjoyed myself."

|

What does it mean to be a "good guest?"
- *To say "Thank you"*
- *To be nice and polite*
- *To be a good friend*

Remind the students that last week they helped Peter understand how to be a good host to Tommy. Today, Peter has just been invited to be the guest in Tommy's home! He needs to learn what to say and do to be a good guest at Tommy's house. Introduce Peter, and use the script to act out the scene:

"Peter the Polite Guest"

Teacher: Hi, Peter. I'm so glad you stopped by today. Did you have a fun time with Tommy at your house last week?

Peter: You bet! I greeted him at the door when he got there—just like we talked about—and I made sure to see him to the door and thank him for coming when he left. We had such a great time that he invited me to his house this week!

Teacher: You sounded a little nervous when we talked yesterday. I told the boys and girls that you needed their help, and they're ready to help. Tell us what you need.

Peter: I'm nervous, and I do need help! Tommy is a new friend, and I've never been a *guest* in his house before. I'm not sure I know what to do.

Teacher: I bet some of the boys and girls can help you. Let's ask, *"Who can tell Peter what it means to be a guest in someone's home?"* (Allow time for the children to respond. If necessary, use the points at the beginning of the lesson to remind them.)

Peter: Is that all there is to being a guest? You just go over to someone's house or join them on an outing? That's easy! I'm going to Tommy's house now!

Teacher: Not so fast, Peter! You said Tommy invited you to come over tomorrow. It wouldn't be *polite* for you to show up before you are supposed to. If you want to be invited back again, you'll need to make sure you are a *polite* guest.

Peter: I do enjoy playing with Tommy. Boys and girls, will you help me learn how to be a polite guest? I really want Tommy and his family to like having me over.

Teacher: We will be happy to help you, Peter! Well, class, what do you think Peter should do when he first gets to Tommy's house? (Take responses from children. If they are still unsure, remind them that Peter

PART 2

doorbell.)   should first knock or ring the

Peter: Yes, ringing the doorbell or
                knocking is the first sign of a
                good guest! I guess that is
                better than just bursting in! I
                will say "Hello" too,
                and I should say it to
                everyone who is there?

Teacher: Yes, Peter, you want to show
                everyone at the house that
                you appreciate the invitation,
                so saying hello when you
                see them is the polite
                thing to do.

Peter: Well, what happens when
                I leave? Do I just walk out, or do I have to say something?

Teacher: Boys and girls, what do you
                think Peter should do when he leaves? (Take responses and discuss that
                he should say "Goodbye" and "Thank you.")

Peter: That's right! I should say "Goodbye" and "Thank you"! Silly me! I will also
                tell Tommy that I had a good time so maybe I could come over and
                play again.

Teacher: Yes, Peter, that is the perfect thing to say! That way Tommy knows how
                much you liked playing at his house.

Peter: Wow, you all have been such a big help! I am really excited to go over
                to Tommy's house tomorrow, and I'm not nervous anymore! Thank you
                and goodbye!

> **Definitions:**
>
> **APPRECIATION**
> Recognizing and
> acknowledging value in
> people, places and things
>
> **POLITENESS**
> Using kind words and actions

After the children say goodbye to Peter, explain to them that even though Peter is going to
visit a friend's house, they should also practice these same behaviors to be a good guest
when they visit anyone's home, whether it is a relative's home or the home of your parent's
friend.

To close the lesson, ask the students to remember what a good guest should do in
someone's home. Ask them to remind you what a good guest would do in the following
situations:

- What do you do when you arrive at the house? (Knock or ring the doorbell.)
- What do you do after someone answers the door? (Say "Hello.")
- What do you do after entering the house? (Say hello to anyone who is there.)
- What do you do when you leave? (Say "Thank you for having me; I had fun!")

|

EXTENDING
CHILDREN'S LEARNING

1. To help students put their thoughts into action, have them enter the classroom as 'your home.' Make sure when they enter that each student knocks and politely says "Hello." At the end of the day, tell the students that now they are leaving 'your home.' Make sure each student knows to say "Thank you" and "Good-bye."

2. Read the Merryville story, "Allie's Party." Afterwards, discuss the ways Allie is a good host along with the ways Caroline improves as a guest. Encourage your students to think about how Allie must feel when Caroline is not being a polite or appreciative guest.

3. Have students draw a picture of themselves being a guest in someone's home. Make sure they explain how they are being a good guest in their picture.

4. Help the children memorize the "Knock, Knock" rhyme as a way to remember the first step for being a good guest:

   Knock, Knock.
   Who's there?
   Hi, hello.
   How are you?

   Knock, Knock.
   Who's there?
   It is _child's name_
   Is _friend's name_ here?

PART 2

Home Connection

Dear Parent/Guardian,

This week we're helping your kindergartner develop the qualities of being a polite guest. Your child is learning that he or she is the guest when visiting in someone else's home and that a good guest is a polite guest. Children are learning the following:

- To knock or ring the doorbell to a friend's home before entering
- To say hello to their friend and any others in the home when they arrive (their friend's parents, siblings, etc.)
- To express their appreciation when leaving by saying "Goodbye. Thank you for having me," or "I enjoyed myself."

Here are some opportunities for you to reinforce your child's development of politeness and appreciation when he or she is the guest:

- Your child may have learned the "Knock, Knock" rhyme to remember the first steps to being a good guest (knocking and saying "Hello!"). If your child learned the rhyme, have him or her teach you; if not, you can teach your child:

Knock, Knock.	Knock, Knock.
Who's there?	Who's there?
Hi, hello.	It is <u>child's name</u>
How are you?	Is <u>friend's name</u> here?

- Role-play arriving at a guest's home with your child:

  - Ask your child to go outside and ring the doorbell. Answer the door and remind your child to say, "Hello, how are you today? Tommy asked me over to play."

  - Ask your child to pretend to leave by walking him or her to the door. Remind your child to say, "Thank you for having me over. I had a great time. Good-bye. Have a good day."

Remember, your child will be watching you to see if you're a good guest when you go places together. Wherever you go, speak to others the way you would want them to speak to you. Be quick to say, "Hello, how are you?" and "Good-bye" with that extra tag—"Have a good day!" Before you know it, your child will be doing the same.

~ From Our Hearts To Yours

ALLIE'S PARTY
PART 1

The last bell of the day had just rung. School was out for the weekend. But this wasn't just another Friday; it was Allie's Friday. Today was her birthday. Three of Allie's friends were coming home with her to get ready for her big party!

Caroline, Jasmine, and Brianna were just as excited as Allie. They'd been talking about the big day all week. Allie had called each one Thursday night to tell them to bring a sleeping bag and pillow because there weren't enough beds in her house to sleep all of them!

When the school bus stopped in front of Allie's house, the four girls jumped off the bus with so much gear they looked like they were going away for the rest of the school year.

Allie's mom greeted the girls at the door and helped them get settled in Allie's room.

"Girls," Allie's mom said, "Put your things in here and then come to the kitchen for a snack."

The girls hurried to the kitchen. Allie helped her mom serve the girls sugar cookies and Kool-Aid, but Caroline didn't want the sugar cookies.

"Allie, don't you have something better than sugar cookies? They're so plain," said Caroline. "Do you have chocolate chip cookies?"

"Let me ask my mom," said Allie. A moment later, Allie reported back, "My mom said we don't have any, but maybe next time you come over we'll have some. Let's go outside and play!"

The girls had only been outside a few minutes, when Caroline groaned, "It's too hot out here. Let's go inside and play games." The other girls weren't ready to go in, but Allie said, "Come on, Jasmine and Brianna, let's go in with Caroline."

The girls went inside and paraded down the hall to Allie's room. Brianna said, "Let's play dolls." But Caroline said, "Dolls are dumb." Jasmine said, "Let's put on makeup." But Caroline said, "Makeup makes a mess." So, Allie said, "Let's paint our fingernails." But Caroline said, "Nail polish stinks."

Allie wanted to help her difficult guest have a good time. She decided it was time to give her friends a special surprise she had made for each of them, a friendship bracelet. Jasmine and Brianna tied their bracelets on their wrists, but Caroline said, "Allie, I don't like the colors in this bracelet. I want another one," as she threw it down on her sleeping bag.

PART 2

Before Allie could say a word, Allie's mom called the girls for supper. They all turned around and ran to the kitchen to see what Allie's mom had made. It was Allie's favorite, spaghetti.

Caroline cried out, "Allie, I thought you said we were having pizza!"

Allie's mom chimed in, "Since it's Allie's birthday, I made her favorite supper as a surprise, instead of pizza." Allie asked her mom to please fix Caroline one of the pizzas she had in the freezer.

After everyone ate their fill of spaghetti and pizza, they brushed their teeth and started getting ready for bed. "Girls, grab your sleeping bags and come to the living room for a movie," said Allie's mom.

It didn't surprise anyone when the movie started that Caroline said, "I saw this movie last week! I don't want to watch it again."

"Caroline, this is the only movie we have. My mom got it just for tonight, so I hope you'll watch it with us," said Allie.

Caroline just complained and pouted. Allie, Jasmine, and Brianna watched the movie and laughed and giggled all the way through. Caroline couldn't stand to watch the other girls having so much fun without her, so she rolled over and went to sleep angry.

After all her guests settled in for the night, Allie turned out the light and tucked in, too.

PART 2

The next morning, the girls woke up to the smell of pancakes cooking in the kitchen. They hurried to the breakfast table wearing their new bracelets...all but Caroline, who still didn't want to wear hers.

After breakfast, Allie's mom said, "Girls, would you mind rolling up your sleeping bags and putting them away before the other guests arrive?"

When Caroline picked up her pillow, she found something she didn't expect. Allie's friendship bracelet was underneath it. Caroline couldn't believe Allie would give away her very own bracelet. Caroline's heart turned from mad to sad.

Caroline thought about what a good host Allie was trying to be. She thought about what a good time everyone else was having. *Maybe it wasn't their fault I've been miserable; maybe it's my fault!*

Caroline was still thinking about how mean she had been when the doorbell rang.

"Caroline, Brianna, Jasmine, the other kids are here," Allie screamed as she ran to the door. Allie opened the door to see not one, but four boys from school standing there.

"Happy birthday, Allie," they all said together. Wesley, Tommy, Terrell, and Jack charged through the door like little knights in shining armor.

"Did you all have a good time last night?" asked Jack.

"Well, Jasmine and I had a good time," answered Brianna.

"What about you, Caroline?" asked Jack. Caroline didn't answer. Instead, she offered to take their gifts and put them on the breakfast table for Allie.

Allie's dad walked in and said, "Guys and girls, welcome to Allie's birthday party. Come out to the backyard, and let's get this party started."

"Thanks, Mr. Roberts," they said as they

ran past him into the big backyard. Even though it was warming up outside, Caroline joined right in. They played dodge-ball and kick-ball and stayed on the run. They played baseball and football and had loads of fun. Even Caroline was laughing and playing. They all played and played in Allie's backyard.

While the rest of the kids kept playing, Caroline walked over to Allie's mom who was putting candles on Allie's birthday cake. "Mrs. Roberts, I'm sorry I was so rude last night. The other girls said your sugar cookies were the best, and I can't believe you gave me pizza instead of spaghetti. Will you ever forgive me?" asked Caroline.

Mrs. Roberts put her arm around Caroline and answered, "Sometimes we all forget our manners. You are very brave to come talk to me. Thank you, Caroline."

"May I help you serve the cake and ice cream?" asked Caroline.

"That would be so sweet of you," answered Mrs. Roberts.

In the meantime, Mr. Roberts gathered all the kids around the picnic table.

"Happy Birthday to you," Mrs. Roberts and Caroline started singing as they walked to the table with the birthday cake lit up with candles. Everyone joined in.

Allie made a wish and blew out all her candles. When they finished eating cake and ice cream, it was time to open gifts.

Caroline gathered all the gifts and handed them to Allie one-by-one. She had as much fun helping Allie as Allie did opening her gifts.

When the party was over, Allie walked each of her guests to the front door.

"Thanks, Mr. Roberts," Wesley said. "I had a great time!"

"The cake was the best, Mrs. Roberts," said Tommy as he hugged Allie to say good-bye.

When it was time for Caroline to leave, she hugged Allie, too. "Allie, I'm so sorry I was so mean to you. You were so nice to me the whole time I was here."

"You're my friend, Caroline, and you were my guest, too," answered Allie.

"Here's your bracelet back, Allie. I can't take it; it's yours," said Caroline. "Caroline, I want you to have it. Now, it's yours," said Allie.

"Happy, Happy Birthday, Allie. This was the best birthday party I've ever been to," said Caroline. "Allie, you're the best!"

JUST THE BEGINNING...

PART 2

Part 3 Communication Skills

Chapter

Greetings and Introductions

I bet you've watched an old *Leave it to Beaver* rerun a time or two. In most episodes, Ward Cleaver walked in the front door of his home after a long day's work to drop his briefcase by the stairs and find his wife, June, for a hello and a kiss. Beaver and his buddies stopped what they were doing to greet 'dad' at the door. Even the obnoxious Eddie Haskell greeted other family members when he came to visit Beaver's older brother, Wally.

Today, kids hardly speak to their parents when either of them walks through the door. If the television is on, no one seems willing to miss a few seconds of the latest episode of 'whatever' to turn and greet their loved one. Too often, we rush to the breakfast table or past the breakfast table without a warm "Good Morning" or "Have a nice day" to our own family members.

What about your students at school? Do they greet the crossing guard? Do they speak to the adults they encounter during the school day? Do they smile or frown when they enter your classroom? Do they say goodbye when they're leaving at the end of the day? Elementary teachers say that many students today do not return adults' greetings. "You say hello to a child in the hall," says one teacher, "and they don't say anything back." Meeting and greeting, like all manners, must be learned.

In this week's lesson, we're going to help you help your students learn how to greet others they meet. Kindergartners will learn how to greet others with a smile and a kind word. First-graders will learn the importance of greeting adults with a smile, eye contact, and a handshake. Learning how to introduce their friends to family members and to other friends will help second-graders develop confidence. Third-graders learn how to make a good first impression.

PART 3

Big Ideas

- A heart-felt greeting builds a bridge to others; not speaking to others builds a wall.
- A smile is a language that everyone understands. When you smile, the world smiles with you.
- Reaching out to others with a warm smile and a friendly hello is the first step in making new friends.
- Learning how to introduce friends to family helps young children overcome shyness and uneasiness in social settings.

Grade-level skills and objectives:

(K) Greeting others with a smile and a kind word is a friendship skill that shows others you are pleased to meet them.

(1) Meeting and greeting adults with a confident smile, a handshake, and a warm greeting shows great maturity.

(2) Introducing friends to family members shows you care about both your friend and your family. Introducing a new friend to a group of old friends shows your new friend how much you care.

(3) Relationships start with first impressions. Making a good first impression builds a bridge to friendship.

PART 3

114 |

Friends-to-Be

Materials and Preparation

Practice the "Hello & Goodbye" song to the tune of "Goodnight, Ladies."

Wilbur's Words of Wisdom

> When you meet a friend once-in-a-while,
> Be sure to greet them with a smile!
>
> A friendly smile
> Seen from a mile,
> That's how we say
> "Come in and Play!"

Guiding Children's Learning

To begin today's lesson, help your students learn the first verse of "Hello & Goodbye." It's sung to the tune of the old classic, "Goodnight, Ladies."

Invite your students to sing with you as you lead the song by going around the room to each student. Look them in the eye with a smile as you sing their name. For example: "Hello, Tommy! Hello, Sue! Hello, Winston! And how are you today?"

First verse:

> Hello, _student's name_! Hello, _student's name_! Hello, _student's name_!
> And how are you today?

Keep going until you've named each child. When you've finished going around the room, the children respond by singing:

> Hello, teacher! Hello, teacher! Hello, teacher!
> And how are you today?

Attributes
Friendliness, Maturity

Kindergarten Skills and Objectives:

Greeting others with a smile and a kind word is a friendship skill that shows others you are pleased to meet them. In this lesson, children will learn the following:

- To meet and greet another child
- To open the heart of another child with a smile and a warm hello
- To smile, so the world will smile back

PART 3

Lead a brief discussion about the importance of saying hello with a smile, using the following questions:

Do you know that you carry a gift with you every day and everywhere you go that you can give others? It doesn't cost anything. It's free and it's a gift that comes back to you. Do you know what it is?

- *A smile*

A smile shows you're friendly. If you were choosing a friend to play with on the playground, wouldn't you choose someone with a smile, not one with a frown?

> **Definitions:**
>
> ***FRIENDLINESS***
> Welcoming others by offering a quick smile and a kind word
>
> ***MATURITY***
> The ability to make the right choice in spite of negative influences

Why is it important to be friendly when you meet someone for the first time?

- *You might make a new friend.*
- *This shows that you care about other people—even people you haven't met!*

Have each student turn to their neighbor to practice a few ways to be friendly when meeting someone for the first time. Walk your students through the following steps:

- Look at the person's eyes.
- Smile.
- Say "Hello, how are you today?"
- State your name and ask theirs: "My name is _____. What's your name?"
- Ask a question and tell something about yourself. (e.g., "Do you like to draw? I do." "Are you new to this school? I can show you around.")

Close by teaching your students the second verse to "Hello & Goodbye."

> *Goodbye, <u>student's name</u>! Goodbye, <u>student's name</u>!*
> *Goodbye, <u>student's name</u>! I'm sad to say goodbye!*

Students respond by singing:

> *Goodbye, teacher! Goodbye, teacher! Goodbye, teacher!*
> *I'll see you here <u>next day</u> (Tuesday, Wednesday, etc.).*

116 |

PART 3

EXTENDING
CHILDREN'S LEARNING

1. Start a new tradition in your classroom. Greet your students with a smile and "Good Morning, _____" as they enter your room. Remind them to respond likewise using eye contact. It won't be long before your students will be greeting you before you have a chance to greet them!

2. Divide the children into pairs. Have one child smile at the other and ask the other child not to smile back. Let them see how impossible it is not to return a smile.

3. Using the "Hello, World" activity sheet, show your students how to write "hello" in languages from around the world. (A good online resource is Google Translate.)

4. Give each student one or more circles of construction paper. Ask them to draw a 'smiley face' in the center of each circle. Encourage your students to look for someone who needs a smile today. Give them their 'smiley face,' and a friendly hello, in addition to a smile on their own face.

PART 3

|

Home Connection

Dear Parent/Guardian,

This week, your child is learning how to politely greet others. Kindergartners are learning the following:

- To meet and greet another child
- To open the heart of another child with a smile and a warm hello
- To smile, so the world will smile back

If you want to avoid coming home to a teenager who doesn't look up from the television to greet you, start now when your child is young to form a habit of speaking to each other when someone enters a room. If you greet your spouse when you come home, your child will pick up on the same behavior. If you speak to your child before you look at the mail or change clothes, he or she will speak to you, too.

You can help reinforce friendly greetings. Try some of these activities at home this week:

- Ask your child to teach you the "Hello & Goodbye" song they learned at school.

- Talk with your child about different ways to say "hello," such as informal greetings (e.g., "Hey, how's it going?") or in other countries (e.g., "Hola!").

- Make it a habit in your home to say "Good Morning" and "Good Night" to each family member.

- Do you remember playing "Stare Down" as a child? You and a friend locked eyes with each other until one of you cracked a smile, laughed or looked away. The stone-faced player was the 'winner.' Play a different version of the game with your child that we call, "Smile Down." Take turns with one of you being the 'smiler' and the other the 'frowner.' The frowner will try not to return the smiler's grin. When the frowner smiles, both of you are 'winners.'

~ From Our Hearts To Yours

|

"Hello, World"

PART 3

Chapter 10

Conversations

Today's students have no memory of a world without cellphones, texting, IMing, computers, and email. Their conversations often take place through the airwaves. Their thumbs have replaced their mouths as transmitters of information. There are no rules to follow. No listening needed. No waiting for a turn. To make matters worse, they 'speak' in code:

- POS-"Parent over shoulder"
- P911-"Parent alert"
- HB-"Hurry back"
- GTR-"Got to run"
- 02-"Your two cents worth"
- !-"I have a comment"
- !!!!-"Talk to the hand"
- BBT-"Be back tomorrow"

But not to fear, there's an SMS Corrector that will automatically translate the text-speak into normal language. Children don't have to learn how to speak in complete sentences; an App will do it for them. I doubt that makes you feel much better as a teacher.

Beyond the obvious difficulties, the greater disconnect is that only 7% of communication is in words; 38% takes place through tone and pitch of voice; 55% of communication is visual. If words are all you have, you only have 7% of your capacity to communicate. No wonder there are so many misunderstandings through electronic communication! No one is fully connected.

Learning to converse accurately and tactfully is a skill that takes practice, face-to-face practice. Our natural bent is to talk for others to listen, rather than listening to others talk. Interrupting is one of the hardest habits to overcome in becoming a good conversationalist. Helping your students master the art of conversation will serve them well in many areas of life. Children who learn the give-and-take of conversing are better students, better friends, and better citizens.

The next Winston Churchill, Susan B. Anthony, Abraham Lincoln, or Martin Luther King, Jr., might be sitting in your classroom this year. Helping your students learn to become engaged in good conversations will help them engage others in bettering our world.

In this week's lesson, kindergartners learn that listening is the first step in having a good conversation. First-graders learn that taking turns makes conversations a two-way connection, not a one-way lecture. Learning how to join a conversation helps second-graders build confidence in group interaction. Third-graders learn that conversations are an opportunity to encourage others with their words.

Big Ideas

- Conversations are an opportunity to connect with others.
- Conversations are as much about listening as talking.
- If you're talking, you're not learning.
- It takes practice to learn to converse well.
- Text-speak should not replace F2F-speak.
- We show others how much we care for and respect them by the way we participate in conversations.

Grade-level skills and objectives:

(K) Listening helps you learn from the person who is talking.

(1) Conversations involve taking turns talking and listening.

(2) Learning how to join a conversation builds confidence.

(3) Encouraging others through your words and gestures makes others want to converse with you.

PART 3

Do you Hear What I Hear?

Materials and Preparation

None

Wilbur's Words of Wisdom

Listening helps us learn!

L Look in the eyes
E End your talking or moving
A Answer questions when asked
R Remain quiet (no interrupting!)
N Nod your head

Guiding Children's Learning

To introduce the lesson, play a game of "Telephone." Divide your class into two groups. Explain the following rules:

- One person from each group will hear the same message and quietly pass it on to their neighbor, who will whisper it to the person next to them, and so on, until all players in each group hear the message.

- When the message has been passed on to each person in your group and the final person hears it, he will whisper what he heard in his ear and then announce what he heard to the class.

- Compare the final messages from each group.

- The goal is to be the best listener you can be so you can pass on the right message!

- This is supposed to be a fun game teaching the importance of listening, so there will be no pointing fingers if someone heard the wrong thing.

Attributes

Participation, Self-control

Kindergarten Skills and Objectives:

Everyone has thoughts, ideas, information, and opinions to share. We show others how much we care for and respect them by the way we participate in conversations. In this lesson, children will do the following:

- Follow five steps to become better listeners
- Follow these steps to show others they are listening

PART 3

|

Designate the direction for students to pass their message on and then play the first round. If time allows, play the game several times, shuffling students so that a new student is at the beginning and end of each line. Use the following sentences or create your own to play:

- "Gracie is a goose."
- "Henry is a tortoise."
- "BillyBeeRight buzzes."
- "Wilbur is an owl."

(NOTE—If you create your own sentence, do not use students' names in the sentences as the misinterpretation could be rather embarrassing.)

Point out to the students that the different response at the end shows them how well they were listening. Use the following questions and comments to guide the students in a continued discussion:

Today we're going to talk about listening during conversations. You probably already listen to some people, like your parents and your friends. Hopefully, you are listening to me right now!

Why is it important to listen?
- *It is nice for the person who is talking.*
- *We can miss important words from the teacher (parent/friend, etc.) if we do not listen.*
- *We can make a mistake if we do not hear what is said.*

There are some behaviors we can practice to help us listen and show the other person that we are listening. (Make sure the students are all looking at you before proceeding.) Let's work on some of these:

- Don't just look at some part of the person who is talking; look in their eyes. (Wait until all students are looking at your mouth or your eyes.)

- Moving around makes it hard to listen and does not show the other person you are listening. (Wait until all students are still.)

- When you are asked a question, answer it! (Ask a few students a question and have them respond to show they are listening. Make sure other students are practicing their listening skills while their classmate is answering.)

- Don't interrupt while the other person is talking. In a conversation, you will both take turns remaining quiet to listen while the other person is speaking. If you need

Definitions:

PARTICIPATION
Choosing to be fully involved in the task or project at hand

SELF-CONTROL
The ability to manage yourself when no one is looking

PART 3

to ask a question from the teacher, you can also remain quiet while raising your hand. (After making this point, look around to make sure students are following the first few steps: looking at you in the eyes, not moving around and remaining quiet. Ask a few students a question while you oversee the listening behavior of the other students.)

- Finally, nod your head to show you are listening and understanding. (Have the students nod their heads.)

- Good job practicing your listening skills! It is very important to know how to listen because it will help you a lot in sharing conversations with others. Not only that, but *listening* helps you *learn* from the person who is talking.

Teach students the following steps to help them remember how to listen and learn:

L Look in the eyes
E End your talking or moving
A Answer questions when asked
R Remain quiet (no interrupting!)
N Nod your head

Close by having students repeat and practice these steps for listening several times with a partner. Explain that if we do not follow these steps, it's easy to either miss what was said or for the other person to at least *think* you missed what was said.

PART 3

EXTENDING
CHILDREN'S LEARNING

1. Practice listening to each other using the steps to 'LEARN.' Any time you or a student is sharing something with the class, encourage everyone to be good listeners by following the five steps.

2. Play "Wilbur Says." The rules are the same as "Simon Says," but use the Wise Ol' Wilbur puppet as Simon. Before you start, remind students of the listening steps so they can do a better job hearing and following what Wilbur says in the game.

3. During a classroom lesson, use a "talking ball." When a child is holding the talking ball he or she can speak while everyone else listens. Stress the importance of listening while someone else is talking. Encourage students to share the ball so they can listen to all class members.

4. At the beginning of the day, tell students that some time throughout the day, you will say the magic phrase, "Merryville." When you say that word, the students who hear it should quietly put their hand on their heart, as if they were going to say the Pledge of Allegiance. The student who hears the phrase first will get the reward of going to recess first that day (or some other equivalent 'prize'). If possible, say the magic phrase in the middle of giving instructions to test how well students are listening.

PART 3

Home Connection

Dear Parent/Guardian,

This week, students are engaging in respectful conversation with others. Kindergartners are learning that listening helps them learn. In class they are being taught the five steps to listening:

L Look in the eyes
E End your talking or moving
A Answer questions when asked
R Remain quiet (no interrupting!)
N Nod your head

You can help reinforce listening skills in direct ways. Try some of these small activities at home this week:

- Set aside an intentional time to listen and talk to your child this week. Take turns telling her stories and listening to stories from her. Encourage your child when you notice her practicing the five steps to listening. Tell her how it made you feel when she listened to you. Ask her how she felt when you listened to her.

- Tell your child about a time when you learned something very important by listening. Tell about another time when you made a mistake because you did not listen well.

- Throughout the week, pay particular attention to times when your child listens well. Thank him for listening at least once each day of the week. Be sure to thank your child for listening during conversations, not just listening to directions.

~ From Our Hearts To Yours

Chapter 11

Telephone Manners

Telephone communication has come a long way.

The prototype for a 'telephon' was made from a hollowed-out beer barrel, sausage skin, and a knitting needle in 1860. Using the same principles, Alexander Graham Bell added electricity and voice transmission to a rectangular wooden box in 1867 to give us the first telephone without a device to signal a call was coming in. A year later a 'thumper' was added to strike the inside of the box to signal an incoming call.

Later, the phone booth was invented to enable a private call in a public area. One could step into the booth, close the door, and shut out the world. The world couldn't hear your conversation, and you couldn't hear the conversations of the world.

In the mid-'60s, Maxwell Smart entertained us with a ringing shoe. Little did we know that crazy spy gadget was actually giving us a glimpse into the not-so-far-fetched cell phone that was introduced in the '70s.

Today, 'thumpers' range from a standard ring to the most obnoxious sounds anyone can imagine. With more than five billion cell phone subscribers walking and talking across the continents, telephone booths no longer shield us from private conversations held in public places.

Are telephone manners obsolete? Hardly! Telephone manners are more important than ever to bring a return of respect and civility to our society. Teaching young children how to answer a phone, make calls, take messages, and carry on a pleasant phone conversation are opportunities to instill respect for others in their hearts. Helping children understand the need to identify themselves when calling a friend's house or the need to speak slowly and clearly into the phone teach children how to think of others ahead of themselves.

In this week's lesson, kindergartners will learn how to answer the phone with polite words and behaviors. First-graders will learn how to speak clearly out of consideration for the caller. Learning how to make a call will help second-graders develop good telephone skills. Third-graders will learn how to take messages and carry on pleasant phone conversations.

PART 3

Big Ideas

- Teaching children telephone manners is much more than teaching them how to make and take calls.
- Expecting children to use the telephone responsibly helps them accept responsibility in other areas of life.
- Helping children understand the perspective of the person on the other end of a call teaches children how to think of others ahead of themselves.

Grade-level skills and objectives:

(K) The first step in developing telephone manners is learning to answer the phone politely.

(1) Telephone manners offer an opportunity for a child to develop consideration for others by learning to speak respectfully to the caller.

(2) Telephone manners offer an opportunity for children to develop polite social skills as they learn how to courteously make a phone call.

(3) Helping children learn to receive and leave messages teaches them responsibility.

PART 3

"Hello, Harris Residence."

Materials and Preparation

- Styrofoam or plastic cups (2 or more)
- 24" string (1 or more)
- Tape

Punch a hole in the center of the base of each cup. Push the string from the outside to the inside of the cup. Tie a knot to hold in place and secure with tape. (Optional—If time allows, you can make enough cup phones for each pair of students.)

Wilbur's Words of Wisdom

When you greet a friendly caller,
Be polite and do not holler!

Guiding Children's Learning

Attributes
Consideration, Politeness

Kindergarten Skills and Objectives:

The first step in developing telephone manners is learning how to politely answer the phone. In this lesson, children will learn how the following:
- How to politely greet the caller
- How to politely ask the caller to wait
- How to politely tell family members when they have a call

Introduce the lesson with a discussion. Use the following questions and comments to guide the students:

Today, we're going to talk about being polite on the telephone.

What does it mean to be polite?
- *To be kind*
- *To be respectful*
- *To be friendly*

Do you think it is important to be polite when you are on the telephone?
- *Yes, it shows others you have good manners.*

PART 3

| **129**

It's very important to be polite when you use the telephone and here's why:

- It makes the other person glad he called.
- It makes the other person feel comfortable.
- It shows the person who is calling that you respect him or her and that you respect the person they are calling for.
- The person calling can't see you, so it's very important that you use polite words and that you do not speak too loudly or too softly.

Now we're going to practice what to say when we answer the telephone.

Definitions:

CONSIDERATION
Taking into account the feelings of others before you speak or act

POLITENESS
Using kind words and actions in all situations

Pick one volunteer to use the other end of your cup phone. Tell your volunteer that he is going to call you, and you are going to answer the phone. Answer the phone using each of the following voices. After each one, ask the students if what you said was a polite and friendly way to answer the phone (or not):

- "HELLO!!!!!" (Yell it.)
- "Hell-ooooo??" (Like you are bored or annoyed)
- "Hello…" (Really quietly)
- "Hello?" (Politely and friendly)

Guide your students through the following role-play activities. Begin each one by showing the appropriate behavior with your volunteer using the cup telephone.

- When you answer the phone, you should say, "Hello, [Harris] residence," in a friendly and clear voice. Turn to your neighbor and practice saying this, using your own last name.

- If the person calling asks for someone else in your home, politely say, "Hold on, please, while I go get him." Try saying this to your neighbor a couple of times.

- Now, when you let your family member know that he or she has a call, do you think you should yell it while you are still holding the phone? (Imitate, "MOOOOOOOMMMMM, PHOOOOOONE!!!" for the class.) No! You should put the phone down and then go tell your family member that he or she has a phone call. Turn to your neighbor to practice politely saying, "Mom, you have a phone call."

- Here's something you may or may not know—While your mom is on the phone, you need to quietly wait for her to finish before speaking to her. Don't interrupt unless it is very, very important!

PART 3

Have students turn to their neighbor to practice the three steps they have learned:

- Politely answer the phone.
- Politely ask the caller to wait while you get the person to the phone.
- Without yelling, get the person for whom the caller is asking.

Close by reminding students of the following:

- Do you remember learning about the Golden Rule? The Golden Rule tells us to treat others the way we want to be treated.
- This is an important rule to remember when it comes to talking on the phone, too! One day, when you start making phone calls, you will want the person who answers to be friendly, not yelling into the phone.
- For that same reason, you should be polite and make sure not to yell when other people call your house.

PART 3

EXTENDING
CHILDREN'S LEARNING

1. Place the cup telephone from the core lesson in one of your learning centers for students to practice politely answering the phone with each other. Be looking for students who need some private reminders or who deserve to be congratulated for their politeness.

2. (NOTE—You will need your students' phone numbers for this activity.) Give each student a "My Phone" activity sheet. Ask them to draw a self-portrait in the square box on their phone and write their name in the writing box below their picture. Give each student their phone number (if it's not already memorized) and have them write the number on their activity sheet. Let the students use their activity sheet to practice dialing and politely calling or answering the phone. Tell students to hang onto their "My Phone" activity sheet for the next extended learning activity.

3. Help your students memorize their phone number using the tune, "Twinkle, Twinkle Little Star." Sing your phone number to the first student and help them sing their number back to you, using the same tune and number from their "My Phone" activity sheet (previous "Extending Children's Learning" activity). Each day for the rest of the week, sing the tune to the first student and then ask them to sing it to the next student down the line.

5 5 5 1   2 3 4   That's my num-ber, now what's yours?

4. Have students enter your classroom throughout the week by saying their polite phone greeting. For example, have them smile while they say, "Hello, Harris residence." You can choose to give a prize to the student who has the most consistent, polite greeting.

Home Connection

Dear Parent/Guardian,

This week we're working on telephone manners. Kindergartners are beginning with the basics by learning how to answer the phone politely. They are learning the following:

- To politely greet the caller
- To politely ask the caller to wait
- To politely tell family members when they have a call

Here are some ways to reinforce your child's development of politeness and consideration on the phone:

- **Teach by example.** Even if you receive an unwanted call, let your child hear you respecting the person on the other line by being polite and considerate.

- **Teach your child not to interrupt when you're talking on the phone.** You'll be teaching more than the first step in telephone manners; you'll be teaching basic patience and respect for others. When guiding your child on this, remember to:

  - Teach your child when it is important enough to interrupt a conversation and when it is not.
  - Teach your child to say "Excuse me" or to place a hand on your arm to indicate he needs your attention, but let him know that loudly saying "Excuse me!" multiple times does not count as politely interrupting.
  - When your child does excuse himself appropriately, indicate you have heard him with a nonverbal cue such as a hand on his shoulder. When it is appropriate to pause the conversation, respond to your child.
  - If you know ahead of time that you will be making a phone call, tell your child you need to be on the phone for a certain amount of time. Ask if he needs anything before you begin. Then tell him that he is not to interrupt you while you are on the phone.
  - Have reasonable expectations. It's not reasonable to expect a five-year-old to wait 45 minutes while you chat if she needs to ask a question. However, it is reasonable for her to give you uninterrupted time to talk with a friend.

- **Give your child lots of practice.** If your child is old enough to answer or make calls, then she is old enough to do it politely and with consideration for the person on the other line. Help your child develop polite telephone skills from the very beginning.

~ From Our Hearts To Yours

My Phone

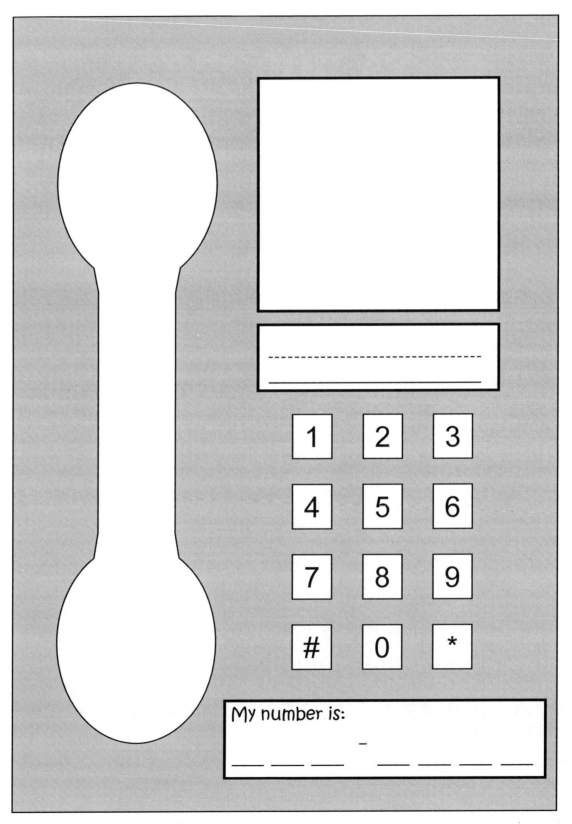

PART 3

Chapter 12

Written Communication

Why is it important to teach children how to master the ancient art of handwritten correspondence in this modern high-tech century? Is it a waste of time and energy? Let's explore the answers to these questions.

Think of why a musician-to-be would choose to master an acoustic guitar before an electric:

- Acoustic guitars have thicker necks, compared to electric guitars which makes it more difficult to play certain chords and reach certain large stretches.
- Electric guitars use thinner strings made of steel, which makes them easier to play than the thicker, bronze, acoustic guitar strings.
- Acoustic guitars have larger bodies than electric guitars, which may cause some difficulty in younger players when reaching for the strings with the picking hand.
- Electric guitars are usually set up with their strings closer to the fret board. This makes it easier to push down the strings, which is less of a strain on a player's fretting hand.
- Acoustic guitars tend to have a higher level of string tension than electric guitars, which makes it harder to push down and hold the strings in place.[1]

It's obvious that learning to play an acoustic guitar is more difficult than playing an electric, so why do it? Students who first learn to play the acoustic guitar have a much easier time when switching over to the electric guitar once they have learned to play.

Helping children learn how to express their deepest feelings in handwritten notes at an early age makes it easier to express themselves as they grow up. Learning the fine art of letter and note-writing makes all other forms of writing much easier. Just as a musician-to-be begins with an acoustic guitar, children need to begin the fine art of writing with handwritten notes, long before they begin writing electronically.

In one of the early books on the subject of writing, Lillian Eichler advised, "When you write to your friends, make your letters so beautiful in form and text that they will be read, re-read, and cherished a long time after as a fond memory."[2]

The letters between Abigail Smith and her husband, our second president John Adams, certainly validate this statement. The following is a beautiful example of a heartfelt closing in a letter from Abigail to John, dated April 16, 1764:

"Adieu, evermore remember me with the tenderest affection, which is also borne unto you by your Abigail."

| 135

I wonder if today's children will have shoeboxes filled with old love letters when they're eighty years old, if all they receive today are text messages. I wonder if today's girls will be able to reflect on their most intimate teenage feelings, if they're using Facebook for what should be diary-only writing. I wonder how boys will learn to show heartfelt gratitude and love, if they're not learning how to put words on paper that express the depth of their emotions.

It has been said that words are the voice of the heart. Teaching your students how to express the voice of their hearts on paper taps into their imaginations. It is from the imagination that all great writing comes.

In this lesson, kindergartners learn to express caring attitudes through pictures without prose. First-graders learn that kind words cultivate deeper friendships. Writing a note of appreciation helps second-graders cultivate a heart of gratitude. Third-graders begin the mastery of handwritten correspondence with the longer task of letter writing.

[1] Read more at <http://www.ehow.com/facts_4926715-easier-learn-acoustic-electric-guitar.html#ixzz1S5aZ7GLI>.

[2] Eichler, Lillian. *Book of Etiquette*. 1922.

Big Ideas

- When you do something thoughtful for someone without expectation of return, you're showing how much you really care.
- The more dependent we become on electronic communication, the more important handwritten communication becomes.
- Learning to express feelings on paper opens the imagination for critical thinking and creative writing.

Grade-level skills and objectives:

(K) Children develop the basics of written communication by making a picture to give away.

(1) Using written words to communicate to others is a friendship skill because it shows we care.

(2) Taking the time and making the effort to send a handwritten note shows someone you are thinking of them.

(3) Writing a letter can be a healthy way to express your feelings while also sharing your thoughtfulness.

PART 3

136 |

A Picture is Worth a Thousand Words

Materials and Preparation

- Plain white paper (1/student)
- Crayons, markers or paint supplies
- (Optional) A picture that a child (outside of class) drew for you

Wilbur's Words of Wisdom

Show others you care
and keep hurts away;
use pictures or words
to share thoughts each day.

Guiding Children's Learning

Begin with a discussion, using the following instructions and questions:

- Today we're going to talk about ways we can show others we've been thinking of them. To do something nice to show you are thinking of someone is to be *thoughtful*.

- When you do *thoughtful* things for other people, you are showing that you care about them and that you are thinking of them. When you do something thoughtful, you make someone else happy, and this makes you happy, too!

- Can you think of a time when you did something to make someone else feel happy? What did you do?

- I bet some of you have made someone else happy by giving them a picture you made. (Optional—briefly share a picture that someone outside of class gave you and how it made you feel.)

- Giving someone a picture you made is a way to show someone else that you're thinking of them—this is one way to show your *thoughtfulness*.

Attributes

Expressiveness, Thoughtfulness

Kindergarten Skills and Objectives:

Children develop the basics of written communication by making a picture to give away. In this lesson, children will learn the following:

- To encourage others through art
- To create a picture to give to someone else

PART 3

|

- Today, each person is going to make a picture for someone else. It's very important to remember that the pictures we make today are not for us.

When would be a really good time to give someone a picture you have drawn or painted?
- *If someone is sick*
- *If someone has a birthday*
- *If you want to say "Thank you"*
- *If you want to say "I miss you"*
- *If you want to say "I love you"*

What picture could you draw for someone who is sick? What should you say to that person?

- *Flowers*
- *Ballons*
- *Hearts*

- *"I hope you feel better!"*
- *"I care about you."*
- *"Get well soon."*

What picture could you draw for someone who has a birthday? What should you say to that person?

- *Presents*
- *Balloons*
- *Cake and ice cream*

- *"Happy Birthday!"*
- *"I hope you have a great birthday!"*

What picture could you draw for someone who does something very nice for you? What should you say to that person?

- *A big happy face*
- *Hearts*
- *Flowers*

- *"Thank you very much!"*
- *"I noticed what you did for me."*

What picture could you draw for someone who lives far away? What should you say to that person?

- *A person waving hello*
- *Two houses far apart*

- *"I miss you!"*
- *"Come back soon!"*
- *"I love you!"*

Do you think giving someone a picture tells them you love them? (Yes!) A picture can also tell people lots of other wonderful things, but most importantly, giving a friend or a family member something that you make shows them that you think of them even when you are not together.

I want you to think of someone who is not in our class for whom you could make a picture. Maybe it's his or her birthday, or maybe someone did something nice for you who deserves a special thank you. Maybe you want to tell someone that you miss them or love them. Think of what you want your picture to say to the person.

Now, it's time to make a picture for that special person!

|

PART 3

Distribute the picture-making supplies to each student. Give students time to draw or paint their picture. If time allows, help children write their name, the recipient's name and a brief description of what the child drew on the back of each drawing.

Close the lesson with the following points while you assist students with their pictures:

- What are some things to remember when we make pictures to give to others? (Walk around the room to make sure they are following these instructions.)
    - *Be respectful in what you draw.*
    - *Write your name on it so they know who it is from.*
    - *Tell the person you are making it for what you drew (painted) for them.*

- It is important to look for times when you can give something, such as a picture, to someone else that will show you are thinking of them.

- Next year and in later years, you will learn how to write a note, a card or a letter to someone to show your thoughtfulness, but a picture is just as good!

Definitions:

EXPRESSIVENESS
Revealing the content of your heart

THOUGHTFULNESS
Looking for ways to make others feel loved

PART 3

EXTENDING
CHILDREN'S LEARNING

1. Read *What Did Loonette Forget? A Book About Being Thoughtful* (Time Life Medical, 1997). Encourage your students to think about what Loonette learned regarding thinking of the needs and feelings of her friends.

2. Make birthday, thank-you or congratulatory pictures as a class for a person at school. Reiterate the importance of using picture-giving to show they are thinking about others. Teach students that the longer they are in school, the better they will become at writing and expressing their feelings through cards or letters for others, in addition to pictures.

3. Have students draw pictures for the people who transport them to and from school. Whether a bus driver, parent or friend, each child can thank an adult for helping them get to school by giving them a picture.

4. Have your students draw a picture for residents of a local nursing home to show the residents that someone is thinking of them. If possible, have students personally deliver their pictures to the home.

PART 3

Home Connection

Dear Parent/Guardian,

This week, we're helping students develop the valuable skill of written communication. While kindergartners are often too young to fully express their feelings through written words, they are still learning the basics by expressing their thoughtfulness towards others by drawing or painting a picture for them.

You can help reinforce your child's development of thoughtfulness in direct ways. Try some of these small activities at home this week:

- Your child is making a picture in class that he is being encouraged to give away. Ask your child who he created the picture for and help him give it away this week. Spend time talking with your child about his picture and what he wants it to say to the recipient.

- Talk to your child about different ways you show others you are thinking of them. Here are some examples:

    - Sending flowers on Mother's Day
    - Writing a letter to an old friend
    - Buying a Valentine's Card for a loved one
    - Writing a card to thank someone for a gift or service

  Point out to your child different times you are doing something special to show someone you are thinking of them or that you appreciate them.

- Kindergartners are not too young to learn the basics of thank-you cards. Teach your child how to express her thankfulness for birthday or Christmas gifts by drawing a picture or writing a card for each person who buys her a gift. Help her to address and mail the picture or card. Help your child remember to do this after each birthday or holiday in years to come!

~ From Our Hearts To Yours

PART 3

| **141**

Part 4 Living in Community

Chapter 13

Respecting Adults

One of the greatest voices of all time, Miss Aretha Franklin, belted out the cry of all of us in her most famous hit song:

 "Oh a little respect. Yeah, baby, I want a little respect.
Now, I get tired, but I keep on tryin.'
Runnin' out of foolin', I ain't lyin'
Yes, respect, all I need is R-E-S-P-E-C-T."

The truth is that most of us spend too much time trying to demand respect and not enough time giving it and, thereby; commanding it. Screaming at a classroom full of children to gain their respect is wasted energy, isn't it? Disrespect begets disrespect…not occasionally, but always.

One powerful lesson in disrespect can be found in political campaigns. Trying to demand respect, candidates too often sideline the real issues to point out the faults and mistakes of their opposition. When politicians fail to recognize their lack of respect for an opponent, it truly says more about the character of the accuser than it does of the accused.

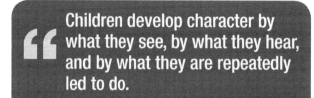

> Children develop character by what they see, by what they hear, and by what they are repeatedly led to do.
>
> -James Stenson

On the other hand, what about those who have learned that respect comes from first respecting others?

- The quiet teacher who rarely raises her voice, but has total control of her students.

- The citizen who doesn't always agree with his elected officials, but chooses to abide by the law without complaint until he can do something to change it.

- The parent who holds her tongue in front of her children. Rather than tear down her spouse or former spouse, she has made the decision to build up the other for the sake of her kids.

When we disagree with a decision made by our school's administration, our community's judge, or our country's president, we have an opportunity to demonstrate honor in front of our children. We should do this through respectful language and obedience to those decisions. However, more often than not, our students hear us complain about the decisions made by those in authority. We shouldn't be surprised when our students have little respect for authority themselves.

As children are surrounded by adults who are respectful of others, they learn how to give respect and earn respect themselves. American author Ralph Waldo Emerson perhaps put this idea most succinctly: "Men are respectable *only* [emphasis added], 'as they respect.'"

PART 4

In other words, for a child to grow into a respectable adult, he must first learn to respect others—beginning with the adults in his life.

In this week's lesson, kindergartners will learn that respect begins in the home with "yes, ma'am." First-graders will gain a greater respect for the adults in their school environment. Showing respect to adults who are keeping their community safe will be the focus for second-graders. The third-graders will begin the process of understanding and respecting the highest positions of authority in our country.

[1] Emerson, Ralph W. "The Sovereignty of Ethics." _North American Review_ X.12 (1878): n. pag. Web.

Big Ideas

- Children find there are many adults in their lives who love and care about them—their parents, grandparents, aunts, uncles, guardians, neighbors, teachers, and friend's parents.
- Children learn they can appreciate the concern of adults by respecting them.
- Children learn that it is important to obey the rules of adults because rules are created to keep them safe.

Grade-level skills and objectives:

(K) Children show honor and respect for parents and other adults by responding politely and promptly to requests and questions.

(1) Adults at school must be respected because they are responsible for making and enforcing rules that keep the school safe, clean, and running smoothly so that every student can learn.

(2) There are many adults in the community who are concerned about children and their safety and must be respected.

(3) Honoring the adults who represent our country demonstrates respect for our country.

PART 4

Yes, Sir - Yes, Ma'am

Materials and Preparation

- "I Don't Understand" (found at the end of the lesson)
- Wise Ol' Wilbur puppet
- (Optional) Recording of the song, "Respect" by Aretha Franklin
- (Optional) Interactive board, white board or chart paper and markers

Wilbur's Words of Wisdom

Adults are older,
Yes, it's true.
More life they've lived
And learned from, too.
They use their skills
To care for you.
So show respect,
It's what they're due.

Guiding Children's Learning

(Optional—Introduce the lesson by playing the song "Respect." Encourage the students to dance and sing while you write R-E-S-P-E-C-T on the interactive board, white board or chart paper.)

Place Wilbur at your side as you introduce today's lesson by reading "I Don't Understand" with great enthusiasm and animation!

After the reading, use Wilbur to lead the children in a discussion about the story. Use the questions and answers below as a guide. Encourage the children to give their own answers first:

What happens the first couple of times Jasmine's mother calls her to breakfast?
- *She does not answer.*
- *She plays a video game.*
- *She does not come when she is called.*

Attributes

Honor, Obedience

Kindergarten Skills and Objectives:

Children show honor or respect for parents and other adults by responding politely and promptly to requests and questions. In this lesson, children will learn the following:

- To respond politely with "Yes, Sir" and "Yes, Ma'am" when answering an adult
- To use appropriate titles for adult family members such as *Aunt* and *Uncle*
- To use eye contact when having a conversation with an adult
- To obey and follow instructions given by an adult

PART 4

Does Jasmine's behavior make her mom upset? Why?
- *It is disrespectful.*
- *Her mom is just trying to feed her a nice meal, and Jasmine does not appreciate it.*

Who watches all this happen, and what do they think?
- *Peter and Penelope*
- *They understand why Jasmine's mother is upset with her.*

Does Jasmine finally understand why her mom is upset?
- *Yes, Wilbur helps her understand.*
- *Yes, she realizes that adults are getting upset with her only after she is disrespectful to them.*

What does Jasmine do differently to start showing respect to her mom?
- *She says, "Yes, Ma'am" when her mom calls her to breakfast.*
- *She comes right away.*
- *She is polite to the adults.*

How does Jasmine feel after she shows respect to her mother?
- *She feels good.*
- *She has a great day!*

Invite the children to name some of the adults in their lives while Wilbur calls attention to the children's use of titles like Mom/Dad, Aunt/Auntie, Uncle, Mr./Mrs., Dr. and so on. Have Wilbur make the following points:

- There are many adults in your life who love and care about you, such as your parents, grandparents, aunts, uncles, neighbors and your friends' parents.

- These adults have been living a long time. They have done lots of different things. They know right from wrong, and they want you to know and do the right thing, too.

> **Definitions:**
>
> **HONOR**
> Valuing the worth of another by showing respect
>
> **OBEDIENCE**
> Choosing to submit to authority

- One way you already show respect for grown-ups is by what you call them and by the way you speak to them. You call adult relatives by names such as Aunt _____ and Uncle _____, and you call your friends' parents by their last names.

Have Wilbur explain to students a few other important ways to show respect for the adults in their lives:

- Look in the eyes of adults when they talk to you.
- Listen with your mouth closed while an adult is speaking.
- Use the right title of the adult who is talking to you (Mr., Mrs., Principal, Aunt, etc.).
- Respond to the adult with "Sir" or "Ma'am."

Teach students **Wilbur's Words of Wisdom** and close by having them practice saying "Yes, Sir" and "No, Sir" to Wilbur.

EXTENDING
CHILDREN'S LEARNING

1. As a class, decide on certain behaviors that are a 'must' whenever an adult is present; this will become your class policy for respecting adults. For example, using card stock, make a sign for each behavior, such as eye contact, mouth closed, Sir and Ma'am. Laminate and attach each sign to a craft stick. Introduce the three signs to your students and remind them of what each represents. Use the signs to remind students about respectful behavior whenever an adult comes into the classroom. When you are not using them, post them in an area where all students can see them.

2. Use Wilbur to help the children practice their new "Respect Rules." Remind students that Wilbur is a grown-up owl. Challenge the children to show him respect as they participate in a conversation with him. Here are some examples:

   - Face Wilbur as he speaks.
   - Listen with mouths closed while Wilbur is speaking.
   - Make eye contact with Wilbur.
   - Respond to Wilbur with "Yes/No, Sir."

3. Read the book *What Do You Say, Dear?* by Sesyle Joslin (HarperCollins Publishers, 1986). This book has silly characters that introduce manners to children. There are appropriate answers for a variety of situations. Have a follow-up discussion about other ideas for being polite, respectful and obedient to adults and others.

4. Do more partner work to practice using polite manners during conversations. Have children take turns pretending to be the adult and the child. Remind students to show respectful behavior toward the 'adult' by looking him/her in the eye, keeping your mouth closed when the adult is speaking, and responding with "Sir" or "Ma'am." Remind children to offer a kind, closing remark at the end of their conversations. Some examples are the following: "Have a great day;" "Thanks for being my partner today," or "You were a great listener!" Some ideas for discussion include favorite foods, pets, television shows, books or vacations.

PART 4

Home Connection

Dear Parent/Guardian,

This week, children are learning to respect adults by responding politely and promptly to requests and questions. Kindergartners are learning the following:

- To respond politely with "Yes, Sir" and "Yes, Ma'am" when answering an adult
- To use appropriate titles for adult family members such as *Aunt* and *Uncle*
- To use eye contact when having a conversation with an adult
- To obey or follow instructions given by an adult

While we know it is important to model respectful attitudes, we can admit we make the mistake of showing a lack of respect for other adults at times. However, honoring and obeying those who possess a greater age or authority than our own teaches children to do the same. When we disagree with a decision made by our school's administration, community's judge or country's president, we have an opportunity to demonstrate honor in front of our children by using respectful language and obedience by following commands given to us without complaint.

To reinforce what your child is learning at school, make some time to talk with your child about ways he or she can show respect to you, your friends and to other adult family members. Kindly help your child remember to show respect in his or her future interactions with adults and do your best to model this same respect toward others.

~ From Our Hearts To Yours

I DON'T
UNDERSTAND

Jasmine woke up and got dressed for school. Her mother called her to breakfast, but rather than coming to the kitchen, she decided to play a video game. Her mother called again, but she didn't answer. Finally, Jasmine's mother appeared at her door.

Peter and Penelope were in the tree outside Jasmine's window waiting to follow her to school.

"Jasmine, it's time for breakfast," her mother said. "I made scrambled eggs and toast."

"I don't want eggs," yelled Jasmine.

"You better work on your attitude, young lady," snapped her mother.

"It's *your* attitude that's the problem, not *mine*," Jasmine snapped back.

Peter and Penelope couldn't believe what they were hearing. They scampered down the tree to wait for Jasmine.

Jasmine came to the table without speaking to her mother, her sister or her brother. After taking just two bites, she pushed her plate away and jumped up from the table.

"I'm outta here," she barked.

"Jasmine, you need to wait on your brother and sister," her mother said. But Jasmine was already out the door to school before her mother could stop her.

"Why is my mother always so mean to me," Jasmine said out loud. "I don't understand."

Peter and Penelope nodded to each other and said, "We understand."

Just a few blocks from her home, Jasmine came to the crosswalk in front of her school. PD and KC were playing with the kids who were waiting for the crossing guard to let them cross the street, but Jasmine didn't want to wait because she wanted to be the first one to school. She darted out of the crowd and started running across the street. The crossing guard blew his whistle and shouted, "Jasmine, STOP!"

But Jasmine didn't stop. She looked back at him and kept running. He kept blowing the whistle. She kept running. PD and KC chased after her.

When she got to the door of the school, she stopped and said to PD and KC, "Why does he only blow the whistle at me? I don't understand." PD and KC understood why.

| **149**

PART 4

Jasmine walked down the hall to her classroom. She sat down at her desk and started talking to Mary. Her teacher, Mr. Smith, said it was time to start the day, but Jasmine just kept talking. He called her by name but she didn't hear him because she was *still* chattering away. Mr. Smith walked over and stood at her desk. She finally looked away from Mary and looked up at him.

"Jasmine, you'll have to stay inside during recess, *again*," said Mr. Smith.

"Why do you always pick on me?" asked Jasmine. "I don't understand."

"Because you're so busy talking, you don't listen," replied Mr. Smith. Turning to her classmates, Mr. Smith said, "Class, let's practice this week's word list."

Jasmine's day was busy with math problems, reading and lots of other stuff, but Jasmine stayed in trouble all day because she talked when she should have been listening.

Jasmine was glad when school ended, and it was time for her soccer game. She really liked soccer. She was fast and had fun outrunning the other kids. In today's game, the coach wanted everyone to have a chance to play. After a few minutes, he called Jasmine, Caroline, and Allie to the sideline. But Jasmine ignored his call and kept playing. He called again, but she didn't listen. He called one more time and then asked the referee for a time out to talk to Jasmine.

"Jasmine, you'll have to sit out the rest of the game for not listening," said the coach. "Until you can learn to listen to me and be a team player, you can't play in the game."

Jasmine kicked the dirt and pouted as she walked off the field. She didn't notice that Wilbur was watching from the trees.

"Jasminnnne," Wilbur hooted. "Peter and Penelope said you might need my help. Come over here and let's talk."

"Wilbur," Jasmine began. "I don't understand why everybody is so mean to me."

"Whooooo's everybody?" asked Wilbur.

"All the adults," answered Jasmine. "My mom, the crossing guard, Mr. Smith, and even my coach."

"Well, let's see," Wilbur said, as he put on his glasses. "Your mother fixed you a good breakfast this morning, didn't she? The crossing guard tries to keep you safe, doesn't he? And I understand you'd rather talk than listen both in class and at soccer."

"Well, I didn't want to stop playing my video game, but my mother made me come to the table…I didn't like it. The crossing guard is too slow. Mr. Smith never lets us talk to our friends. The coach wants to be fair to everybody, but I'm the best player."

"Well, Jasmine," answered Wilbur, "It seems to me your day would go a whole lot better if you showed adults a little respect. They have a hard time helping you when you don't respect them."

"But, Wilbur," Jasmine started.

Wilbur interrupted, "Jasmine, just try giving them respect. That will change everything!"

Jasmine went home mad at Wilbur and everyone else. But the more she thought about what Wilbur said, the more it made sense. Maybe there was something to the idea of respecting others that she was missing.

So the next day, Jasmine answered, "Yes, Ma'am" and came downstairs for breakfast the first time her mother called. Her mother

PART 4

was thankful for the new attitude. Jasmine felt better, too.

When Jasmine saw the crossing guard, she told him good morning and waited for his signal before she crossed the street. It was great not hearing his whistle blow.

Jasmine was the first one to answer, "Yes, Sir," when Mr. Smith was ready to start class. He noticed and smiled at her. Jasmine sat up taller in her desk.

All day long, Jasmine remembered what Wilbur told her about respecting adults. She couldn't believe how different the adults acted around her. At soccer practice, Jasmine even told her coach she was sorry about not listening the day before. She felt much better.
On her way home from soccer practice, Wilbur swooped down and said, "Jasmine, tell me about your day."

"Oh, Wilbur," Jasmine said. "I really tried to show respect all day long. Guess what? I had a great day!"

"Now, you understand," Wilbur said with a wink. "We have to respect others the way we want to be respected!"

JUST THE BEGINNING...

PART 4

Chapter 14

Respecting the Team

In our individualistic society, we teach children how to compete but often neglect to teach them how to cooperate. A highly competitive youngster who doesn't learn the joy of cooperation will sooner or later become a loser, not a winner, because being a winner is much more than finishing first.

Being a real winner is giving others credit for your win. Not hogging the ball, but sharing opportunities to make the score. Building up teammates who need encouragement. Showing respect to the other team's players, coaches, and parents. Accepting a win with humility. Accepting a loss with grace.

Most of us have watched in awe as Olympic athletes from all over the world compete for the gold. The level of competition is unparalleled. The level of respect is equally unparalleled. Did you know the "Golden Rule" of the United States Olympic Committee (USOC) is "real athletes show respect?" According to the USOC, "Real athletes show respect for *themselves*, for their *teammates*, for their *competitors*, and for their *sport*. They are courteous and conduct themselves with dignity." Olympians are expected to "congratulate their opponents on their victories, to always do what is right, to obey the rules of competition, to behave on the field in a way that others will admire, and to maintain a positive attitude."[1]

As exciting as the spirit of competition may be in the Olympic Games, the spirit of cooperation is considered just as important by the participants. The best example of true cooperation in competition was witnessed during a Special Olympics race. The children were nearing the finish line when the lead runner tripped and fell to the ground. The competitors had been instructed during training to keep going if someone was injured. They were taught that a trainer would come to the aid of an injured runner. However, their hearts wouldn't allow them to pass by another runner who had fallen. With a show of great respect, they picked him up, locked arms, and crossed the finish line together.

This lesson will help children develop an 'Olympic-sized' respect for their teammates *and* their competition....on and off the field. Kindergartners will learn the joy of cheering others on. First-graders begin to understand that playing fair is more fun. In second-grade, students will learn how to think of the needs of their teammates ahead of their own. Finally, third-graders will develop the skills of sportsmanship.

[1] Visit <http://www.teamusa.org/resources/u-s-olympic-education/real-athletes-show-respect> for more information on the expectations of our Olympic athletes

PART 4

Big Ideas

- In today's society, we often teach children how to compete but neglect to teach them how to cooperate.
- A highly competitive youngster who doesn't learn the joy of cooperation will sooner or later become a loser, not a winner.
- When children show respect for their team, they develop a cooperative spirit that displays good sportsmanship and selfless interaction with others.

Grade-level skills and objectives:

(K) Waiting for your turn and cheering for your teammates develops selflessness and a team spirit.

(1) Playing by the rules and learning to play fair are keys to good sportsmanship.

(2) Striving to be a valuable team player puts the good of the team ahead of yourself.

(3) A good sport wins well and loses well.

PART 4

|

Your Turn First

Materials and Preparation

- Peter and Penelope puppets

Write "Wilbur's Kindness Pledge" on your classroom board or chart paper.

Wilbur's Words of Wisdom

Wilbur's Kindness Pledge

Today I pledge to wait my turn,
To put others first so I can learn.
Today I pledge to encourage friends;
It's how you play, not who wins.

Guiding Children's Learning

Today's lesson will utilize a relay race for students to participate in a team sport. Before beginning, review the following rules for the relay to ensure that the game is fun and enjoyable for everyone:

- Everyone participates.
- Wait your turn; don't get ahead of a teammate.
- No pushing or shoving.
- Encourage and cheer for teammates by using kind words (e.g., "Awesome!" or "Way to go!").

Use our Peter and Penelope relay or another cooperative team game. Procedures for the Peter and Penelope relay follow:

1. Divide your class into two equal teams and provide each team with a Peter or Penelope puppet.

2. Have each team form a single-file line.

3. Give a Peter or Penelope puppet to the person at the front of each line.

4. The person at the front of the line must pass the puppet *over* his head to the person behind him. The next person in line must pass the puppet *under* her legs

Attributes
Cooperation, Selflessness, Sportsmanship

Kindergarten Skills and Objectives:

Selfishness keeps many children from becoming good team players. Waiting for your turn and cheering for your teammates develops selflessness and a team spirit. In this lesson, children will learn the following:

- To wait patiently for their turn while playing games in a group
- To offer encouraging words to their teammates
- To exercise sportsmanship during a game

PART 4

to the person behind her. This should continue with students passing it either over their head or under their legs until the last person receives the puppet and says, "Peter/Penelope is home!" (Make sure students know which puppet name to say at the end of the relay.)

5. The first team to finish the relay wins.

6. If time allows, change directions and do the relay again. Remind students to use kind words and gestures as they play.

After the relay, lead a brief discussion about how the children worked as a team. Introduce terms such as *selfless, cooperation, and sportsmanship* in your discussion, if appropriate. Give specific examples of positive behaviors or words during the relay. Use the following questions and comments:

- How did it feel to work together with your classmates?
- Is it more fun to play with others than to play by yourself?
- Sometimes it is hard to wait for your turn, but when you wait your turn, you're being a good ("**selfless**") teammate.
- I heard some of you cheering for your classmates. Did it feel good to help them play their best? That's **cooperation**!
- When you care more about how you play than whether you win, that shows good **sportsmanship**. For example, sportsmanship is when you say, "We didn't finish first, but that's okay. We still had fun! Let's play again."

Close the lesson by teaching children "Wilbur's Kindness Pledge." Have them recite the pledge. Keep it posted where children can see it and be reminded. Refer to it when necessary and point out examples of ways children are selfless, patient with their friends, cooperative with one another and encouraging.

Definitions:

COOPERATION
Working with others for everyone's best; choosing to be helpful, not hurtful

SELFLESSNESS
Choosing to give of yourself with no expectation of return or consideration of loss

SPORTSMANSHIP
Being more concerned with supporting your team than helping yourself

PART 4

EXTENDING
CHILDREN'S LEARNING

1. Introduce board games such as *Candyland, Chutes and Ladders or Bingo* to small groups of children. Help them come up with a fair way to determine who goes first: rolling dice for the highest number, the tallest or shortest or alphabetically by name. Remind students to be patient while waiting their turn and to use supporting and encouraging words when others have to "Go Back" or lose a turn.

2. Introduce card games such as *Go Fish, Old Maid or Battle*. Monitor sportsmanship during the games and remind the students how to respond to each other after the game is over. Give them appropriate responses. Here are some examples: Winners say, "Good game. I enjoyed playing with you." or "Thanks, that was fun." Losers say, "Good game." "Congratulations." "Nice win." "Thanks for playing with me." After students become better at being gracious winners and losers, they will come up with their own encouraging words and phrases.

3. Throughout the rest of the year, before your students play a game, have them recite "Wilbur's Kindness Pledge" to be reminded that it's more important how you play than whether or not you win. Have them teach their kindness pledge to school personnel and/or other classes of students.

4. Choose one or more books from the list below to read aloud to the students. Afterwards, discuss the importance of teamwork and sportsmanship:

   - *Elf Help for Kids' Playing Fair: Having Fun* by Daniel Grippo (Abbey Press, 2010)
   - *Clifford's Sport Day* by Norman Birdwell (Cartwheel Books, 1996)
   - *Arthur's Teacher Trouble* by Marc Brown (Little, Brown and Company, 1989)
   - *Three Wishes* by Lucille Clifton (Bantam Doubleday Dell Publishing Group, 1993)
   - *Mean Soup* by Betsy Everitt (Houghton Mifflin Harcourt, 1995)
   - *Jamaica Tag-Along* by Juanita Havill (Houghton Mifflin Harcourt, 1996)
   - *Amazing Grace* by Mary Hoffman (Dial Books, 1991)
   - *Playing Fair* by Shelly Nielsen (Abdo & Daughters Publishing, 1992)

Home Connection

Dear Parent/Guardian,

In this week's lesson, students are learning how to be good teammates. Kindergartners are playing games and reciting "Wilbur's Kindness Pledge," which teaches them the following:

- To wait patiently for their turn while playing games in a group
- To offer encouraging words to their teammates
- To exercise sportsmanship during a game

You can help your child develop sportsmanship and cooperation in direct ways. Here are some activities to reinforce what your child is learning at school:

- Have a Family Game Night. Once a week, play board games or card games with the whole family. Remember to encourage your child to use supportive words and to let others go first. Shake hands or high-five at the end of your games to practice good sportsmanship and to demonstrate gracious winning and gracious losing!

- Your child is learning "Wilbur's Kindness Pledge" this week. Make copies of the pledge below and ask each family member to sign it. Post the pledge on your refrigerator or in a prominent place in your home as a reminder to the whole family of what it means to be a good team player.

Wilbur's Kindness Pledge

Today I pledge to wait my turn,

To put others first so I can learn.

Today I pledge to encourage friends;

It's how you play, not who wins.

_____
(NAME)

_____
(DATE)

~ From Our Hearts To Yours

PART 4

|

15

Respecting Differences

When you were a child and someone passed by who looked different from you, what did your mother *always* say? "Don't stare, honey." So, you looked the other way. "Don't stare" became "don't look." The problem—"Don't look" then became "don't see."

Throughout my grade school years, my mother taught a Sunday School class for adults with limited abilities. Two of my mother's students sat with us during the worship service that followed. Carol, who was in her thirties, suffered brain damage during her traumatic birth and had great difficulty keeping quiet, making odd noises that often interrupted the silence of the sanctuary.

Carol liked sitting next to me. I didn't mind sitting next to Carol. Mother taught me to reach over and squeeze Carol's hand when she made inappropriate sounds. Almost without exception, at least once every Sunday, I would gently squeeze her hand as a reminder that she needed to tell herself to be quiet.

One particular Sunday, I was the one having trouble sitting still in the pew. Unexpectedly, Carol reached out and squeezed my hand as a signal for me to settle down. When I looked in her eyes, she winked with a nod of understanding. She let me know she knew how hard it was to stay quiet and sit still through an entire service.

With that look, Carol taught me a life-transforming lesson that day that I've never forgotten. On the inside, we're much more alike than different, no matter how much we may differ on the outside. Wouldn't it be wonderful if we could understand that we have much more in common with each other than we have differences, no matter how extreme the differences appear to be? Wouldn't it be wonderful if we could respect each other's differences as qualities that make us unique rather than traits that make us unusual?

In preparing this lesson, we consulted with The Arc, a well-respected national organization that promotes and protects the rights of people with intellectual and developmental disabilities. During our first meeting, we presented the outline for the lessons, which included the attributes of acceptance and compassion. Our eyes were opened when the executive director pointed out that compassion would be the wrong attribute in building respect for those with differences. As he explained, "Compassion is only one step away from pity, and pity is the last thing that *anyone* wants or needs."

He's right, isn't he? The truth is we're all different. None of us needs pity; rather, we need *acceptance* and *understanding*.

In these lessons, we hope to open the eyes of your students' hearts to understand that no matter how many differences we see on the outside, we all have the same needs on the inside.

|

PART 4

Big Ideas

- Treating those who are different with respect means understanding we may look different or act different on the outside, but we all have the same heart needs on the inside.
- Showing pity for someone who is different only makes them feel different.
- Offering acceptance regardless of differences makes others forget their differences.
- Understanding differences as the qualities that make each of us unique opens children's hearts to accept others for who they are.

Grade-level skills and objectives:

(K) Children recognize differences and similarities in others with acceptance and understanding.

(1) Young children who develop the ability to look at others with the eyes of their hearts are able to see past differences in those with disabilities.

(2) We can learn something from everyone—regardless of age, young or old—and in turn, we can help them learn, too.

(3) When we learn the customs of other cultures, our world grows bigger. When we share our customs with others, we help their world grow bigger, too.

PART 4

You're Different, Just Like Me

Materials and Preparation

None

Wilbur's Words of Wisdom

Friends may come
in all looks and smarts;
What matters most
is the size of their hearts.

Guiding Children's Learning

Introduce the lesson by playing a game called "Find a Friend Who_____?"

The students will mingle around the room looking for specific qualities in their classmates. Sometimes the qualities will be different and sometimes the qualities will be the same. Give them these instructions:

- I will tell you to look for something that is the *same* or *different* in another classmate, and you will need to look for a student who matches this description.
- When you find another student who has the same or different quality as you, stand together as friends. You can find only one partner.
- Sometimes, you may not be able to find someone who matches what you're looking for. That's okay. Stand by yourself until the others are finished.
- Before you move on to finding a new partner, I want you to shake hands and thank your partner.

After you read each quality, emphasize whether students are looking for something that is the same or different in another student. Here are some qualities for them to look for:

- Find a friend who has the same color shoes as yours.
- Find a friend who has the same color shirt as yours.
- Find a friend who is a lot taller, or a lot shorter than you.
- Find a friend who has the same skin color as you.

Attributes
Acceptance, Understanding

Kindergarten Skills and Objectives:

In this lesson, children distinguish the differences and similarities in others with acceptance and understanding. Children will learn the following:

- To recognize similarities in others
- To recognize differences in others
- To focus on similarities rather than differences in others

PART 4

- Find a friend who has the same number of brothers and sisters as you.
- Find a friend who has a different pet than you.
- Find a friend who has the same favorite food as you.
- Find a friend who has a different hair color than you.
- Find a friend who has the same eye color as you.
- Find a friend who has a different favorite color than you.
- Find a friend who drinks the same thing you drink at lunch.
- Find a friend who lives in your town.

When the game is complete, lead a group discussion using the following questions:

Did you have trouble finding a friend?
- *Yes, I couldn't always find someone like me.*
- *Yes, not everybody looks like I do or likes the same things I do.*

How did it feel when you could not find a partner?
- *Disappointing*
- *Sad*
- *Lonely*

How did it feel when you did find a partner?
- *Fun*
- *Exciting*

Do we play only with people who are the same as us?
- *No. If I only play with someone like me, someone will be left out.*
- *No. If I only play with someone just like me, I'll be alone.*

What are some similarities that we all have?
- *We all have eyes and hair and skin, even if they are different colors.*
- *Nobody likes being left out.*
- *Nobody likes playing alone all the time.*

> ## Definitions:
>
> ### ACCEPTANCE
> Treating everyone you meet with the same respect, regardless of differences
>
> ### UNDERSTANDING
> Looking at others and listening to others without judgment

What did you learn about finding new friends?
- *If I always look for others who are like me, I'll miss a chance to make a new friend.*
- *If I always play with others who are just like me, I'll hurt the feelings of those who are different from me.*
- *If I always look for others who are just like me, I'll end up playing alone.*

Close by teaching students **Wilbur's Words of Wisdom**; if desired, teach them your own hand motions. Explain that when we look at others with the eyes of our *hearts*, we care more about their qualities on the *inside* (e.g., that they are a good friend, that they are funny, that they are kind) than we care about what they look like on the *outside* (e.g., the color of their hair or skin).

PART 4

EXTENDING
CHILDREN'S LEARNING

1. Take a picture of each child's face and arrange them together on one page. Print the page on cardstock and laminate. Cut the page into a puzzle. In a small group center, have the children put the puzzle together. When all groups have completed the puzzle, discuss that each child is a different piece of the puzzle. Also, each puzzle piece is part of the same picture and is of equal importance, just like each of them. Follow up with regular puzzles from the class or do online jigsaw puzzles. (Visit www.jigzone.com for more ideas.)

   As a modification to save time, simply write the first and last name of each student on cardstock, making sure to have the names somewhat close together for making the puzzle.

2. Read *Unlovable* by Dan Yaccarino (Owlet Book, 2004). As you read, stop and discuss Alfred's feelings when the other animals see only his differences. Continue to read and stop at different places and have the children talk about what might happen next. At the end of the story, discuss how Alfred made a new friend *before* seeing that friend behind the fence. Alfred became friends with Rex without meeting him face to face because he knew Rex's heart.

3. Play a variation of "Simon Says" that we call "Wilbur Says," using your Wise Ol' Wilbur puppet. Tell the students that not everyone can respond to all of Wilbur's commands; some students will respond to each command and some will not. Have all students stand up while you use Wise Ol' Wilbur to give commands that are appropriate for your class. For example: "Wilbur says, 'Everyone with brown eyes stand on one foot.'" "Wilbur says, 'Everyone whose favorite sport is football raise your right arm.'" "Wilbur says, 'Everyone who has a pet dog pat your head'" and so forth. When you decide to stop, have the students sit down and share one thing they learned about another student. Focus on similarities, differences and the acceptance of both.

4. Read *The Crayon Box That Talked* by Shane DeRolf (Random House, 1997). Illustrated in every color in the crayon box, the simple message comes through that when we all work together, the results are much more interesting and colorful than when we work alone.

   Open a new box of crayons and spill them on a table top so the children can see all the colors. Ask the following questions:

   How are the colors the same?
   - *They're all made from wax.*
   - *They're wrapped in paper.*
   - *They 'live together' in the same box.*
   - *They were made at the same time in the same place with the same machines.*
   - *They're the same size.*

PART 4

How are the colors different?
- *They're each a different color. No two are the same color.*
- *They become different sizes when they are used.*

Help your students think about how their class is like a box of crayons and how each one of them is like a crayon that contributes something different, but important, to your classroom. (Throughout the year, look for opportunities such as this that will stretch your student's cognitive understanding, in addition to supporting their appreciation for differences in others!)

Recommended Reading List*
- *Leo the Late Bloomer* by Robert Kraus (Harper Collins, 1994)
- *Rolling Along: The Story of Taylor and His Wheelchair* by James Riggio Heelan (Peachtree Publishers, 2005)
- *We'll Paint the Octopus Red* by Stephanie Stuve-Bodeen (Woodbine, 1998)
- *I Have a Sister, My Sister is Deaf* by Jeanne Peterson (Harper-Collins, 1984)
- *When I Grow Up* by Candri Hodges (Jason & Nordic, 1994)
- *What's Wrong With Timmy?* by Maria Shriver (Little, Brown Books, 2001)
- *Don't Call Me Special: A First Look at Disability* by Pat Thomas (Barron's, 2002)
- *Words Are Not for Hurting* by Elizabeth Verdick (Free Spirit Press, 2002)
- *Special People, Special Ways* by Arlene Maguire (Future Horizons, 2000)
- *Brianna Breathes Easy: A Story about Asthma* by Virginia Kroll (Albert Whitman, 2005)
- *Susan Laughs* by Jeanne Willis (Henry Holt, 2000)
- *Nathan's Wish: A Story about Cerebal Palsy* by Laurie Lears (Albert Whitman, 2005)
- *Taking Asthma to School* by Barbara Mitchell (Jayjo Press, 1998)
- *The Crayon Box That Talked* by Shane DeRolf (Random House, 1997)
- *Unlovable* by Dan Yaccarino (Owlet Book, 2004)

Many thanks to our friends at The Arc for their book suggestions.

Home Connection

Dear Parent/Guardian,

In this week's lesson, kindergartners are learning to focus on similarities in others, rather than differences. Wilbur taught them the following:

> **Friends may come
> in all looks and smarts;
> What matters most
> is the size of their hearts.**

Your child's teacher explained that when we look at others with the eyes of our hearts, we care more about their qualities on the *inside* (such as their friendship, their sense of humor, their academic success or their kindness) than we care about what they look like on the *outside* (such as the color of their hair or skin).

Try this activity at home to support your child's understanding and appreciation of differences in others:

1. Gather your family into the kitchen to help every member learn a valuable lesson about how much we all need each other.

2. Use your favorite cookie recipe and work together as a family with each member taking part in the process. Each person can contribute something different to the recipe (taking turns with each step.)

3. Talk about the importance of each person's contributing something different to the cookies and that each ingredient is different, but of equal importance, in making the cookies. You cannot leave out flour or sugar, for example, and still make a good cookie.

4. Mold each cookie into a different shape and then cook them. (Use cookie cutters if you like or just your hands.)

5. While you are eating the cookies, talk about the fact that they all look different but taste the same and are still good cookies. Relate the cookies to the similarities and differences within your own family while focusing on similarities being more common than differences.

~ From Our Hearts To Yours

Chapter 16

Respecting Others' Rights

When elementary students were asked why kids bully, they didn't say it was because the bully doesn't feel good about himself. They said a bully bullies because "he wants to get his way" or because "he likes pushing other kids around." They told us a bully bullies because "she thinks bullying will make her popular."

Could it be that the kids are right? Bullies bully because they'd rather be mean than nice? They'd rather be in charge than be a team player? They want others looking at them instead of looking at someone else? Kids tell us bullies are full, not empty. Full of the wrong stuff, with no room left for the right stuff.

The responses to our high school program have given us great insight into the world of bullying. A former participant in our *Leaders by Example*® program called my name as I was leaving a local restaurant one evening. When I turned around, I saw a high school fellow with a big grin on his face standing in front of me. "I gotta' tell you something," he said. "I was a 'bad dude' before you came along. You gave me a reason to straighten up. You expected a lot from me because you believed I could be better. Oh, and I love you, too, Miss Jill."

Did you hear the secret that turned this 'bad dude' from a bully into a buddy? He responded to someone who loved him enough to expect more from him. His troubled heart opened to the possibility that he could be so much more than a bully.

The actions of a seven-year-old who's pushing his classmates around are coming from a troubled heart—a heart filled with anger and disappointment. A heart locked for self-protection. It's often true that kids growing up without feeling loved can't love others; children love as they are loved. Love is the key that unlocks hearts, emptying out the bad stuff and allowing the good stuff to get in…transforming a bully into a buddy. The good news is, you can help your students feel loved and learn to love others.

In this week's lessons, we help children develop empathy, the ability to feel the pain of others within their own hearts. We help children recognize ways they hurt others and what to do about it. We help children gain the courage to help their classmates who are being bullied by stepping in and standing up! Also, we help children help their classmates turn away from hurting others to helping others.

|

Big Ideas

- Children demonstrate kindness for others when they care about the feelings of others.
- Empathy is feeling the pain of others in your heart.
- Children learn how much better it is to be a buddy than to be a bully.

Grade-level skills and objectives:

(K) Children learn to show kindness by helping and sharing.

(1) Children realize there is much to be learned by listening to the opinions of others. Interrupting others keeps you from making friends.

(2) Children learn they have a choice—to be a buddy or a bully.

(3) Children begin to understand they have a choice to make—to stand back and watch someone being bullied or to step in and stand up by offering help.

PART 4

What's Mine is Yours

Materials and Preparation

- "The Little Red Hen" (found at the end of the lesson)

Wilbur's Words of Wisdom

Don't be a *bully*; be a buddy!

Guiding Children's Learning

Begin by reading "The Little Red Hen" (original version can be found at the end of the lesson). Lead a brief discussion about the characters and their unwillingness to show kindness, to share or to put the needs of others before their own. Ask the following:

Do the animals in the story think about the needs of the Little Red Hen, or do they think only of themselves?
- *Only of themselves. They will not help Little Red Hen make the bread.*
- *Only of themselves. They want to eat Little Red Hen's bread, even though they did not help her to make it.*

Do the animals show they care for one another? How could they have shown the hen they care for her?
- *They could have helped Little Red Hen make the bread.*

How do you think Little Red Hen feels when no one helps her make the bread?
- *Lonely*
- *Sad*
- *Angry*

Do you think this story shows how to make friends?
- *No. (It shows how not to make friends.)*

Attributes
Empathy, Kindness

Kindergarten Skills and Objectives:

Through the story of "The Little Red Hen," children will better understand how others feel when we are unkind. In this lesson, children learn the following:
- To make friends by helping
- To respect the rights of others by sharing

PART 4

How do you act when you want someone to be your friend? What kind of things do you do?

- *You are kind.*
- *You are helpful.*

Do you think Little Red Hen should have shared her bread, even though the other animals do not help her make it?

- *Yes. It still would have been kind for her to share.*
- *Yes. Maybe they will help next time, if she shares with them this time.*
- *Yes. Sometimes, all it takes is someone to show some kindness for another person to be kind.*

How does it feel when your friends don't share with you?

- *Bad*
- *Hurts my feelings*

Conclude the lesson with these reminders:

- It makes us feel good when others help us. We need to remember this by helping others whenever we have the chance.
- It makes us feel good when others share with us. We need to remember this by sharing with others whenever we can.

Teach students **Wilbur's Words of Wisdom** by saying the cheer and clapping twice. They can repeat this several times. Make this your classroom reminder to be kind at all times!

> # Definitions:
>
> **EMPATHY**
> Walking in another person's shoes
>
> **KINDNESS**
> Showing care and consideration in an unexpected and exceptional way

|

EXTENDING
CHILDREN'S LEARNING

1. Divide your students into two groups. Have half of your students act out the story "The Little Red Hen" as it was told. Then, have the rest of the students act out the story as it *should* be told, with the other animals helping Little Red Hen make the bread and with Little Red Hen sharing her bread at the end.

2. Divide your students into small groups to make a trail-mix snack, called chicken feed. Let each group divide up the jobs for making the snack—one person measures ingredients, another adds ingredients to a zipper-type bag, another seals the bag and shakes, and another prepares the table for eating. When they are finished eating the snack, bring the class together to debrief. Ask the following:

   - Did everyone in the group help out?
   - How did it feel to wait your turn to help?
   - How did you behave differently from the characters in *The Little Red Hen*?
   - Why is it important to help and to share with others?

3. Display four jump ropes and four hula-hoops. Explain that there are not enough toys for everyone to have one at the same time. Ask the children to come up with a fair way to share the toys. Allow children to try out their ideas and then discuss how well they worked. Close by reminding them to always come up with creative ways to take turns since sharing is an important part of being a buddy.

4. Read *The Rainbow Fish* by Marcus Pfister (North-South Books, 1992). Afterwards, present a container of colored, fish-shaped crackers to the children and have them come up with a fair way of dividing the crackers. Place blank, fish-shaped paper in your classroom's library or writing areas where children can draw ways to demonstrate kindness and sharing. Combine pages to create a book. Have children come up with a title, decorate a cover using sequins to represent fish scales and then place the book in the classroom library.

PART 4

Home Connection

Dear Parent/Guardian,

This week, your child is learning how to respect the rights of others. Kindergartners are learning how to be a "buddy" and not a "bully" by helping others and by sharing. Here are some opportunities to reinforce your child's continued development of kindness and empathy:

Plan giving opportunities. Have your child make something such as a baked good, a picture or a card for someone who needs cheering up. Talk with your child about how that person might feel after receiving the gift.

Be an example. Let your child see you sharing and taking turns.

Set expectations for your child. Prior to the arrival of a friend, talk with your child about sharing and taking turns. Make your expectations clear and remind your child that a good host is considerate and puts the needs of his guest before his own.

Help your child see the impact of sharing and putting the needs of others first. Call attention to the way in which your child's behavior positively affects her guests. This will likely encourage her to repeat the behavior. Use simple statements like, "Did you see the big smile on your friend's face when you shared your toys? I think she had a good time."

Model and role-play how to share and take turns. If necessary, give your child words to use to help her learn to take turns: for example, "Tell your sister that you would like to have a turn. Say, 'When you are finished, I would like to play with the toy.' Now you try it."

Review the Golden Rule often. When your child has trouble sharing or taking turns, remind her of a time when others didn't share or take turns with her. This will help her to shift her focus from herself to others and how they feel.

Set rules and consequences. Some children, in spite of all your efforts, have difficulty sharing and taking turns. Set one or two simple rules (such as, "Don't say, 'You can't play' or 'You can't have a turn'") and consequences for not following the rules. Be consistent in enforcing the rules and consequences.

~ From Our Hearts To Yours

170 |

THE LITTLE
RED HEN

Little Red Hen found a grain of wheat.

"Who will plant this?" she asked.

"Not I," said the cat.

"Not I," said the goose.

"Not I," said the rat.

"Then I will," said Little Red Hen.

So she buried the wheat in the ground. After a while, it grew up yellow and ripe.

"The wheat is ripe now," said Little Red Hen. "Who will cut and thresh it?"

"Not I," said the cat.

"Not I," said the goose.

"Not I," said the rat.

"Then I will," said Little Red Hen.

So she cut it with her bill and threshed it with her wings.

Then she asked, "Who will take this wheat to the mill?"

"Not I," said the cat.

"Not I," said the goose.

"Not I," said the rat.

"Then I will," said Little Red Hen.

So she took the wheat to the mill where it was ground.

Then she carried the flour home.

"Who will make me some bread from this flour?" she asked.

"Not I," said the cat.

"Not I," said the goose.

"Not I," said the rat.

"Then I will," said Little Red Hen.

So she made and baked the bread.

Then she said, "Now we shall see who will eat this bread."

"We will," said cat, goose, and rat.

"I am quite sure you would," said Little Red Hen, "if you could get it."

Then she called her chicks, and they ate up all the bread.

There was none left at all for the cat, or the goose, or the rat.

| **171**

PART 4

Chapter 17

Respecting Others' Privacy

Gossip used to be a nasty little word that described a nasty little habit. But in today's world, gossip has become big business that pays big bucks. Just stand in the grocery store line, and you'll get your fill of it in the headlines of the magazines. Flip through the television channels, and you'll hear all you never wanted to know about 'you know who.' We can't seem to get enough of it.

In a world filled with gossip columnists, tell-all television shows, and Internet chat rooms, how can you begin to help children understand that gossip is still gossip...hearsay and falsehoods, mean-spirited and harmful? We believe you begin by teaching children to respect the personal space of others.

In this week's lesson, we set in place the foundational understanding that despite what they see and hear, it is important for children to respect the privacy of others. We encourage kindergartners to knock before entering a room. We help first-graders leave the belongings of others alone, even when no one is looking. Second-graders learn to recognize the difference between tattling for the wrong reasons and reporting for the right reasons. Third-graders take a deeper look at how to choose their words carefully, so they build others up rather than tear them down with unkind gossip.

Big Ideas

- Understanding the importance of personal space helps children develop maturity in respecting others and respecting themselves.
- Respect is shown not only in front of others, but behind their backs, too.
- Showing respect for the privacy of others tells others that you are trustworthy.

Grade-level skills and objectives:

(K) Developing consideration for others begins with understanding personal space.

(1) Learning to respect the private space and the personal belongings of others—especially when no one is looking—helps children develop a sense of right and wrong behavior.

(2) Understanding the difference between tattling and telling helps children learn to share information about others for the right reasons.

(3) Learning how gossip hurts everyone—the one who is talked about and the one who is doing the talking—helps children choose their words carefully.

Don't Burst Their Bubbles

Materials and Preparation

- Bubbles (1)
- Hula-hoop (more than one would be most helpful)

Wilbur's Words of Wisdom

Respect his place; it's personal space!

My Hands and My Shoes

I'll keep my hands to myself, and my feet in my shoes.
I'll keep my hands to myself and I won't bother you.
I'll keep my hands to myself so you can take a snooze.
I'll keep my hands to myself, 'cause it's the right thing to do.

Guiding Children's Learning

Use bubbles to introduce the lesson on privacy and personal space. As you blow bubbles, have the children observe what happens to them (e.g., float to the ground and burst, bump other bubbles and burst, or connect to other bubbles when they touch). Invite the children to share their observations before making the following point:

- You each have an area around you that is all your own. It is called your *personal space* and is similar to a bubble.

Give students a visual representation of *personal space* by having one child stretch his arms out to the side and turn slowly. Explain that all the area around the child—the space to the sides of, in front of, and behind him— is considered his *personal space*.

Walk slowly towards the child as he continues to turn and have the other students guess what will happen. Explain the following:

Attributes
Consideration, Trustworthiness

Kindergarten Skills and Objectives:

Developing consideration for others begins with understanding personal space. In this lesson, children will respect the privacy of others by remembering the following:
- Honoring others' personal space
- Keeping hands and feet to themselves
- Knocking before entering a room

PART 4

- Sometimes people enter another person's personal space and someone gets hurt.
- Entering someone else's personal space when you are not invited is similar to "bursting their bubble."
- You can show respect for others and their privacy by staying out of their personal spaces and keeping your hands and feet to yourself. That means no touching, poking, pushing, or pulling on classmates.
- Remember, your personal space is a space just for you. Others should not enter it unless you give them permission to enter.
- Entering someone's room without knocking is disrespecting their personal space.
- Sometimes, you will need to be very close to others, such as when you are waiting in line, or sitting in a group. This is not the same as entering someone's personal space. However, when you are trying to bother someone with your hands or feet, this is disrespecting their personal space. You are "bursting" their space bubble.

Now, pass a hula-hoop around the room from one student to the next. Let each one stand in the middle of it, reach down, and lift it over his/her head to better understand what the personal space of others looks like. After the hula-hoop exercise, teach students a new rhyming song on respecting the personal space of others:

My Hands and My Shoes

I'll keep my hands to myself and my feet in my shoes.
(Move hands to hips, then stomp feet.)

I'll keep my hands to myself, and I won't bother you.
(Move hands to hips, shake head back and forth. Then, point to neighbor.)

I'll keep my hands to myself so you can take a snooze.
(Move hands to hips; then clasp hands beside cheek, pretending you're asleep.)

I'll keep my hands to myself, 'cause it's the right thing to do.
(Move hands to hips. Then, nod head up and down while pointing finger.)

Remind your students of today's lessons learned:
- It's important to respect the personal space of others.
- Keep your hands and feet to yourself so you don't disturb the personal space of others.
- No touching, poking, pulling, or pushing another person.
- No entering without knocking.

PART 4

EXTENDING
CHILDREN'S LEARNING

1. Play *Personal Space* tag. Give each child a hula-hoop to wear and identify one child as "It." Explain that when you give the signal, the children are to run because "It" is going to try to invade their personal space by tagging their hoop with his hoop. If successful, the child tagged becomes the new "It." Also, explain that children must avoid bumping into one another's hoops while running. If they do, they are out of the game, must drop their hoop, and sit in the center of it until the next round.

2. Using the "Door Hanger" template, help your students make a door hanger to give to a family member. Help them write "Please Knock." They can then decorate it with stickers and color it. Remind your students they should always knock before entering someone's room. This door hanger will help them to remember.

3. Read and discuss *Personal Space Camp* by Julia Cook (National Center for Youth Issues, 2008).

4. Partner your students so they can practice knocking before entering. Ask children to stand on opposite sides of one of their desks. Instruct one child to "knock" on their desk and say, "May I come in?" before they move to the other side of the desk.

5. Read the Merryville story "Who Said You Said?" Afterwards, lead a discussion about the importance of respecting the private conversations of others. Ask the students how they would have felt if someone listened to their private conversation and told others the wrong story about what happened.

Definitions:

CONSIDERATION
Taking into account the feelings of others before you speak or act

TRUSTWORTHINESS
Doing what you say you're going to do when you say you will do it

Home Connection

Dear Parent/Guardian,

This week, your child is developing more consideration for others by understanding the meaning of personal space. Your child is learning to honor the personal space of others, to keep his hands and feet to himself and to knock before entering a room. Children are learning the following song:

My Hands and My Shoes

I'll keep my hands to myself and my feet in my shoes.
(Move hands to hips, and then stomp feet.)

I'll keep my hands to myself, and I won't bother you.
(Move hands to hips, shake head back and forth. Then point to neighbor.)

I'll keep my hands to myself so you can take a snooze.
(Move hands to hips; then clasp hands beside cheek, pretending you're asleep.)

I'll keep my hands to myself, 'cause it's the right thing to do.
(Move hands to hips. Then, nod head up and down while pointing finger.)

Here are some opportunities for you to reinforce what your child is learning about respecting the privacy of others:

- Talk with your child about maintaining an appropriate *personal space* around different individuals—family members, close friends, teachers and/or strangers. Together, choose a key word or phrase your child can use when she feels her personal space has been invaded by someone else.

- Call attention to or have your child count signs, such as "Do Not Enter," "No Trespassing" or "Private" when you are in public places. Discuss the importance of safety and respect for the privacy of others.

- Help your child make a door-knob hanger that says, "Please Knock" for a room in your home. It can be two-sided with "Come In" written on the other side. Help your child to remember this family rule and to respect the privacy of other family members by knocking first.

- Model your own respect for the privacy of others by knocking before you enter your child's room.

~ From Our Hearts To Yours

Door Hanger

|

PART 4

WHO SAID
YOU SAID?

Nobody in Merryville can make an apple pie that comes close to Mrs. McDonald's happle pie. Lots of folks make apple pies, but Mrs. McDonald is the only one who can make a happle pie, a secret recipe passed down through the ages. It's always crispy on the outside and extra tasty on the inside. In the springtime Mrs. McDonald keeps the kitchen windows at the Farm wide open when she's baking those pies. The smell of fresh happle pie can be smelled up and down Main Street.

Today is baking day at the Farm. It won't surprise you that Wise Old Wilbur is sitting on the kitchen window sill visiting with Mrs. McDonald while she's baking. Nobody in Merryville loves the smell of happle pies the way Wilbur does.

Mary's coming by to pick up a pie for her Granny who just loves the taste of a fresh happle pie.

"Good Morning, Wilbur," Mary said as she stepped on the porch of Mrs. McDonald's house.

"It's a good morning, indeed," answered Wilbur.

"Good Morning, Mary," said Mrs. McDonald. "I have a happle pie ready for your Granny. I added a little extra of my special extra goodness for her. I know how much she loves my pies."

"She sure does, Mrs. McDonald," said Mary. "She's always telling everybody how great your pies are!"

Mrs. McDonald chuckled and said, "Mary, be sure and tell your Granny, I think she's great!"

"I'll do it," answered Mary. "Have a good day baking!"

"Bye, Wilbur. You have a good day, too!" Mary said as she headed back to her Granny's.

Carolina the Cow was munching grass in the pasture near the porch and overheard what Mrs. McDonald said.

Carolina walked over to Helen the Horse and said, "I can't believe Mrs. McDonald thinks that Mary's granny is always late!"

"Well, that's not a nice thing to say, but maybe she's right," thought Helen.

Since it was a very hot day in Merryville, Helen clopped down to the pond to get a cool drink. Gracie the Goose was there enjoying an afternoon swim.

"Gracie," said Helen, "Did you know that

|

PART 4

Mary's granny broke Mrs. McDonald's pie plate?"

"Do tell," answered Gracie. "Why in the world would Granny break Mrs. McDonald's pie plate?" wondered Gracie as she swam to the other side of the pond.

Freddie the Frog was sunning on his lily pad when Gracie swam by. "Freddie, did you know that Mrs. McDonald broke granny's garden gate?"

"Oh, know," croaked Freddie. "Granny loved her garden gate." Freddie stretched back on his pad to catch a few more sun rays, but he couldn't stop thinking about how upset Granny must be about her broken garden gate.

Penelope the raccoon was sitting on an old log near the edge of the pond. She had just finished eating a snack, so she was washing her hands, as raccoons always do.

"Hey, Freddie," said Penelope. "What are you up to today?"

"Penelope, I'm worried about Mary's granny," answered Freddie.

"Why, what happened?" asked Penelope.

"You didn't hear?" asked Freddie. "Mrs. McDonald said Mary's granny is so overweight, she can't get through her garden gate!"

Penelope couldn't believe Mrs. McDonald would say such a nasty thing about Mary's granny. "Why that doesn't sound like something Mrs. McDonald would ever say," thought Penelope.

Penelope was so upset that she ran to find her brother, Peter, to ask him what to do. She found him resting in his favorite tree outside Granny's kitchen window.

"Peter," called Penelope. "I'm so upset I don't know what to do. Mrs. McDonald is telling people all over Merryville that Granny is so overweight, she can't get through her garden gate." Penelope didn't notice that Granny's kitchen window was open.

Granny stuck her head out the window and hollered, "What *did* you say, Penelope?" just as Mary walked through the kitchen door with Mrs. McDonald's fresh happle pie in her hand.

"Well, why I never," exclaimed Granny as she grabbed the happle pie from Mary and stormed out the door for Mrs. McDonald's house. She was really, really mad that Mrs. McDonald would say such an awful thing about her.

Mary tried to stop her, but couldn't. Mary thought she knew what happened along the way, so she went straight to Penelope.

"Penelope, who told you what Mrs. McDonald said?" asked Mary.

"It was Freddie the Frog," answered Penelope.

Mary went straight to Freddie the Frog.

"Freddie, who told you what Mrs. McDonald said?"

"It was Gracie the Goose," answered Freddie.

Mary went straight to Gracie the Goose.

"Gracie, who told you what Mrs. McDonald said?"

"It was Helen the Horse," answered Gracie.

Mary went straight to Helen the Horse.

"Helen, who told you what Mrs. McDonald

said?"

"It was Carolina the Cow," answered Helen.

Mary went straight to Carolina the Cow.

"Carolina, who told you what Mrs. McDonald said?"

Carolina replied, "I heard it with my own two ears as I was munching my grass."

Meanwhile, Granny passed a lot of folks on the way to Mrs. McDonald's. She thought everybody was looking at her like she was big as a house. By the time she got to Mrs. McDonald's, she wasn't nearly as mad as she was sad.

Mrs. McDonald saw Granny coming with the pie, so she ran to the porch to greet her dear friend, not knowing she was mad and sad. "Is something wrong with the pie?" asked Mrs. McDonald.

"How could I eat THIS pie, after what you said?" snapped Granny.

Mary ran up, "Wait! Wait! I can set the record straight," she said to the two upset ladies.

"Mrs. McDonald, Freddie said you said, 'Granny's so overweight she can't get through her garden gate.'

And Gracie said you said, 'Mrs. McDonald broke Granny's garden gate.'

And Helen said you said, 'Granny broke Mrs. McDonald's pie plate.'
And Carolina said you said, 'Granny's always late.'

But what you really said was that you think Granny's great!'"

"Oh, Mrs. McDonald," Granny said as she hugged her dear friend. "I knew you wouldn't say that awful thing about me, even if I do eat too many of your happle pies!"

"Seems to me…there's too much gossip in Merryville these days," Mrs. McDonald said shaking her head. "Let's go in and have a cup of tea and a slice of pie."

"Yes, indeed," Granny agreed.

JUST THE BEGINNING...

PART 4

Chapter 18

Respecting Property

Do you know the property rules of a toddler?

- If I like it, it's mine.
- If it's in my hand, it's mine.
- If I can take it from you, it's mine.
- If I had it a little while ago, it's mine.
- If it's mine, it must never appear to be yours in any way.
- If I'm doing or building something, all the pieces are mine.
- If it looks just like mine, it's mine.
- If I saw it first, it's mine.
- If you are playing with something and you put it down, it automatically becomes mine.
- If it's broken, it's yours.[1]

Unfortunately, in today's world these property rules extend well beyond the toddler years. I'm sure you're dealing with them every day in your classroom, in the hallways and maybe even in the teachers' lounge!

We all have the tendency to like what isn't ours.

This week, we help children begin to understand the importance of respecting property—whether that property is their own or whether it belongs to someone else. To begin, kindergartners learn to respect shared areas by cleaning up their messes. First-graders learn the importance of taking care of their belongings by putting them away after use. In second grade, students learn how and why they should care for the belongings of others. Finally, in third grade, students respect the intellectual property of others by learning not to cheat and not to take credit for someone else's work.

[1] Author unknown. Found online at <http://www.opt.indiana.edu/clinics/pt_educl/bv_peds/toddler.htm>.

Big Ideas

- Others will respect your belongings only if you respect your belongings.
- Treat your belongings the same way you would like to be treated.
- Treat the belongings of others the same way you would want them to treat your belongings.
- If you're the one that opens it, it's your job to close it.
- If you're the one that spills it, it's your job to clean it up.
- If you're the one that takes it, it's your job to put it back.
- Cheating is hurtful both to the person being cheated and to the person doing the cheating.

Grade-level skills and objectives:

(K) Children learn responsibility by cleaning up their own messes.

(1) When children are responsible for picking up after themselves, they learn to appreciate their space and possessions.

(2) Showing respect for the property of others helps children learn to take responsibility for their actions.

(3) Children learn to appreciate the work of others and the importance of doing their own work honestly.

PART 4

If You Spill It... Clean It Up!

Materials and Preparation

- Cup of water (1)
- Crackers (2-3 total)
- Paper towels
- Small sweeper and dust pan

Wilbur's Words of Wisdom

No matter the address
When you make a big, ol' mess,
Don't leave it or distress.
Clean it like it was, no less.

If You...
(Borrowed by Wilbur from Cap'n Nick)

If you open it, close it.
If you turn it on, turn it off.
If you unlock it, lock it.
If you spill it, clean it up.
If you take it out, put it back.
If you break it, fix it.

Guiding Children's Learning

In today's lesson, we're teaching children the importance of taking responsibility for their actions by cleaning up after themselves to instill appreciation for those who clean up after us at home and at school.

If your classroom includes learning centers, create a mess in one of your centers. (Hopefully, this can be done in the absence of your students. We would hate to model wrong behavior for them!)

If you do not use learning centers in your classroom, create a mess with crackers and a cup of water by crumbling the crackers on the floor and spilling the cup of water.

Now, begin the lesson by showing the children the mess. Then, walk away from it and ask the following questions:

Attributes
Appreciation, Responsibility

Kindergarten Skills and Objectives:

Children show responsibility by cleaning up their own messes. In this lesson, children will learn the following:
- To clean up after themselves
- To offer to help others clean up
- To take care of toys and furniture
- To keep their classroom organized and clean

PART 4

Why do you think I left the mess and did not clean it up?
- *You did not feel like cleaning it up.*
- *It was too much work to clean up.*

Have you ever felt like leaving a mess for someone else to clean up?
- *Yes, because I was tired.*

Do you usually wait for someone else to clean up your mess, or do you clean it up yourself?
- *I let someone else clean-up for me.*

Do you ever offer to help others clean up their mess, even if it was not your fault?
- *Sometimes*

What could happen if I don't clean up my spilled water?
- *Someone could slip on it.*

Why is it important to clean up your spills or messes?
- *To keep someone from getting hurt*
- *To keep others from having to clean it up*
- *To show respect for those around me*
- *To show respect for the furniture or the floor, which cost money*

What could happen if you don't clean up a spill or a mess?
- *Someone could fall and hurt themselves.*
- *Messes can get sticky and smell really bad.*
- *A spill could ruin the floor, carpet or furniture if it is not cleaned up.*
- *Bugs!*

Who cleans up at school?
- *The janitor*
- *The teacher*

Should the janitor or teacher clean up for you when you make a mess?
- *No, I should always help clean up my own messes.*

Now, choose two volunteers to help you clean up your mess! Focus on these actions:

- Say "I'm sorry, it was an accident" after you make the mess.
- Immediately start cleaning up your mess.
- Have your student volunteers offer to help clean up the mess as well, by saying, "Let me help you."

Teach children Cap'n Nick's "If You" chant by saying the first part of each line and having students repeat the responsible behavior (e.g., You say, "If you open it;" they say "Close it!"). Repeat the chant several times, getting faster and faster, until it becomes easier for the students to remember.

Definitions:

APPRECIATION
Recognizing and acknowledging value in people, places and things

RESPONSIBILITY
Following through on your duties without supervision

PART 4

EXTENDING
CHILDREN'S LEARNING

1. Set up a restaurant in the home center. Have each child take on a job. You will need a cook, waitress, busboy/girl, cashier and a customer. Let them pretend to cook food. Make sure they all do their own jobs as they role-play the situation. Guide the students toward being respectful of the person who cleans the tables. At the end of the activity, make sure they all work together to clean up the restaurant using real or pretend brooms, mops and wipes, and putting away all kitchen items.

2. Each day before lunch, remind students what they have learned about cleaning up after themselves. Monitor them in the lunch room, having them take turns wiping the tables and offering to help out by picking up any stray napkins or other messes.

3. When cleaning up a center, play music or sing a song that is an appropriate length for cleaning. Let them know that only by working together will they be able to get the job done before the song is over.

4. Use Cap'n Nick's "If You" chant to create a classroom policy on everyone's responsibility to clean up after him/herself. When needed, gently remind students of what they are supposed to do if they open it, turn it on, unlock it, spill it, take it out or break it. Repeat the chant with students each morning until the words are memorized.

If You...
(Borrowed by Wilbur from Cap'n Nick)

If you open it, close it.
If you turn it on, turn it off.
If you unlock it, lock it.
If you spill it, clean it up.
If you take it out, put it back.
If you break it, fix it.

5. Read "Tommy Tripper's Trouble" (found at the end of the lesson) to your class. Afterwards, lead a discussion about the importance of respecting the property of others and what happens when Tommy does not take care of the property of others.

|

PART 4

Home Connection

Dear Parent/Guardian,

Children begin to demonstrate responsibility by cleaning up their own messes. This week, kindergartners are learning the following:

- To clean up after themselves
- To offer to help others clean up
- To take care of toys and furniture
- To keep their classroom organized and clean

Children are being taught...

If you open it, close it.
If you turn it on, turn it off.
If you unlock it, lock it.
If you spill it, clean it up.
If you take it out, put it back.
If you break it, fix it.

Here are some opportunities for you to reinforce what your child is learning about respecting property:

- When you are out, encourage your child to pick up trash when he is walking and put it into the next trash can he finds. (Next time you are walking into a store you can easily apply this lesson in the parking lot.)

- Set a good example by picking up and wiping up after yourself.

- Set up rules about rinsing a dish and putting it into the dishwasher. It takes longer to get things done, but if you encourage your child to help with cleanup at home, he/she will be more appreciative and will learn to share in other responsibilities as they grow older.

- Have child-friendly clean-up supplies (vinegar and water in a small squirt bottle) on hand to encourage your child to help with chores. Encourage your child to help with messes that are not her fault so she learns to assist others in cleaning up their spills. Make sure that basic supplies are within reach.

~ From Our Hearts To Yours

| **187**

If You...

If you open it, close it.

If you turn it on, turn it off.

If you unlock it, lock it.

If you spill it, clean it up.

If you take it out, put it back.

If you break it, fix it.

Cap'n Nick

|

PART 4

TOMMY
TRIPPER'S TROUBLE

The second-grade class of Merryville gathered at the lighthouse one day to listen to Cap'n Nick tell one of his famous stories. Sometimes he told stories from his days on the high seas. Sometimes he told stories that he made up in his imagination. Sometimes he told stories to teach a lesson. Today, he told a story about the day Tommy Tripper left all the doors open behind him, and everything went wrong in Merryville.

So Cap'n started the story…

Tommy Tripper's dad was trying to fix up some things at the Trout Farm, but he didn't have one of the right tools. He had one kind of wrench, but he needed another kind. He knew Ol' McDonald probably had the tool in his barn, so he sent Tommy over to fetch it.

"Tommy, be sure to ask Mrs. McDonald if you can borrow a wrench from the barn. I'm sure she won't mind, but don't forget to ask," said Mr. Tripper.

"Sure thing, Dad. I'll be back before you know it," answered Tommy as he sped off on his bike.

In a flash he was at Mrs. McDonald's door. He knocked twice and opened the door as he called out her name, "Mrs. McDonald, it's Tommy. My dad needs to borrow a wrench from the barn."

"Come on in, Tommy. That's fine with me. Go on out to the barn and get what you need," said Mrs. McDonald. "You can grab a cookie on your way out."

Tommy grabbed a fresh, warm cookie as he raced out the back door to the barn.

The barn door was closed, but Tommy knew how to slide it open. Inside was every tool anyone could ever need. Tommy looked around awhile trying to find the one his dad needed. He finally saw it, but it was out of reach. He grabbed a paint can to stand on, so he could reach the wrench. He ran out the barn door as fast as he could because he knew his dad was waiting.

Tommy was in such a hurry that he didn't know the paint can turned over and spilled bright blue paint all over the barn floor. Tommy ran across the yard and hollered, "Thanks, Mrs. McDonald, for the wrench

|

and the cookie," as he unlocked the side gate and jumped on his bike to speed back to Tripper's Trout Farm to take the wrench to his dad.

"Now, this is when the trouble started," added Cap'n Nick. "Because, you see ..."

Tommy had gone in the front door without closing it behind him. He'd gone out the back door and left it open, too. Tommy had even slid the barn door open, but hadn't closed it either. Then, when he had jumped on his bike, he'd left the side gate open.

So, Sketch the Skunk went in the front door. KC the Cat went in the back door. Gracie the Goose went in the barn, and Carolina the Cow walked out the side yard and down the street.

Sketch the Skunk was sniffing around Mrs. McDonald's house. Sketch scared Mrs. McDonald, and she screamed. Mrs. McDonald scared Sketch. When he gets scared, he stinks up the place. Sketch ran out the door. Mrs. McDonald wondered how in the world Sketch got into her house.

Suddenly, Mrs. McDonald heard a crash in the back of her house. She ran into the kitchen to find KC licking up spilled milk from a broken glass on the floor. "KC, what have you done? How did you get in my kitchen?" asked a very upset Mrs. McDonald. She clapped her hands and shooed him out the back door.

When she looked up, she saw Gracie the Goose waddling out of the barn. She became even more upset when she saw the big blue gooseprints Gracie was leaving behind. She ran to the barn and found a puddle of bright blue paint all over the barn floor. Before she could grab Gracie, Gracie was waddling through the open side gate, headed straight downtown.

Then, Mrs. McDonald turned and realized

Carolina the Cow was not in the side yard. In the distance she heard Carolina mooing a happy moo. "Oh, no," she thought, "I bet Carolina found her way to Miss Charlotte's Chocolate Shop. She just loves Miss Charlotte's milk chocolate."

Mrs. McDonald ran out the side gate and down the street. She followed Gracie's gooseprints all the way to the mayor's office. The mayor was holding Gracie with a scowl on his face. He had bright blue paint all over his new suit.

"Moooo, Moooo," sang Carolina the Cow from the Chocolate Shop. Mrs. McDonald ran across the street with Gracie under her arm to stop Carolina from eating any more milk chocolate.

Mrs. McDonald apologized to the mayor and Miss Charlotte for all the mess Gracie and Carolina had made.

Just then, Tommy Tripper came down the street on his way to Miss Charlotte's. His dad had given him a quarter for his help, and he was going to spend it in the Chocolate Shop.

When Mrs. McDonald saw Tommy, she realized all the troubles started after he had been at her house that morning. "Tommy, did you close the front door after you opened it this morning?" asked Mrs. McDonald.

"Uh, no, ma'am. I guess not," Tommy said in a quiet voice.

"And, Tommy, did you close the back door when you went out to the barn?" Again, "Uh, no, ma'am. I guess not," he said in a quieter voice.

"Tommy, did you close the barn door when you left the barn?"

"Uh, no, ma'am. I guess not," Tommy said

in an even quieter voice.

"And, Tommy, did you lock the side gate when you left the side yard?"

"Uh, no, ma'am. I guess not," Tommy whispered.

The mayor chimed in and said, "Tommy, maybe you'll never forget that if you open it, you close it. If you spill it, you clean it up. If you unlock it, you lock it, and if you take it out, you put it back. And, I would suggest when you take back Mrs. McDonald's wrench, you clean up the spilled paint and Gracie's gooseprints all along the way. Is that a deal?"

"Yes, sir," answered Tommy. "I won't let this ever happen again. I promise!"

So, Cap'n Nick turned to the class and said, "I hope you learned the same lessons from this story that Tommy learned in real life…

> If you open it, close it.
> If you turn it on, turn it off.
> If you unlock it, lock it.
> If you spill it, clean it up.
> If you take it out, put it back.
> If you break it, fix it.

JUST THE BEGINNING...

PART 4

Chapter 19

Respecting Your Community

Have you ever felt embarrassed by the behavior of your students on class outings? Has the disrespectful behavior of your students been enough of a problem to deter class field trips? Many teachers complain that kids today don't know how to behave in public places, but if kids aren't learning basic civility at home or at school, how can they be expected to behave appropriately when they are out in their community?

Today, civility is commonly considered 'a thing of the past.' In our fast-paced society, it is easy to think we simply don't have time to practice many of the old-fashioned courtesies once deemed essential. However, our communities function more smoothly, efficiently, and pleasantly when both children and adults practice common respect for others.

> **"** **Education comprehends all that series of instruction and discipline which is intended to enlighten the understanding, correct the temper, and form the manners and habits of youth, and fit them for usefulness in their future stations.**
>
> -*Webster's* (1828)

Taking the time now to teach our children civil behavior will save a great deal of time and frustration in the future. Parents who make time to practice table manners at home raise kids who also know how to behave in restaurants. Teachers who expect respectful behavior in the classroom find their students live up to these same expectations in public places. In fact, teachers who have used our curriculum most frequently comment on the difference they see in their kids on class outings, even being thanked by staff at the zoo or the museum for bringing such civil students—We know it can be done!

In these lessons, we help children understand the importance of civility—of acting "respectfully" in social situations. Kindergartners will learn to behave appropriately in social gatherings by using basic manners. First-graders will practice their civility skills for the movie theater. Second-grade students will learn how to exercise respectful behavior in restaurants. Finally, third-grade children will be challenged to think about civility at the mall.

PART 4

|

Big Ideas

- Civility—acting respectfully around others—shows respect for others in your community.
- Our communities function more smoothly, efficiently, and pleasantly when both children and adults practice common respect for others.
- To have respectful communities down the road, we need to reinforce respectful behavior in the classroom today.

Grade-level skills and objectives:

(K) Civility begins with acting respectfully at social gatherings.

(1) There are respectful behaviors to practice even in fun places—such as the movie theater!

(2) Practicing civility when eating out creates a better dining experience for everyone.

(3) Using civility at the mall shows maturity and builds trust between children and adults.

PART 4

Social Graces for Social Places

Materials and Preparation

- Large jar
- "Just Act Respectful!" activity sheet—with the different scenarios cut and placed in the jar

Wilbur's Words of Wisdom

Public place, use inside voice,
Wait nicely in long lines.
Mind crowded spots
Always smile lots—
Civility is kind!

Guiding Children's Learning

Begin by explaining that today you will talk about respecting your community through civility. Define civility as acting respectfully around others. Then, teach children Wilbur's civility poem (shown above). Have them practice saying it several times.

Introduce the *JAR*—a jar with scenarios inside for discussion. *JAR* stands for "Just Act Respectful"! Using the "Just Act Respectful" jar, continue with a discussion about civil behavior at social gatherings. One at a time, pull a scenario out of the JAR and ask students to tell you what the civil or "respectful" behavior would be in that scenario. Explain that some of these situations are a review from past lessons. Let them act it out, when appropriate. Here are the different scenarios:

- If you see someone drop something, you should...
- If you get a present from a friend at your birthday party and you already have one, you should say_____.
- If you are eating with others and you are finished with your meal, you should...
- If you don't like the food being served, you should...
- When a guest is leaving, you should say _____.
- Show me the kind of voice you should use if you are at a gathering with friends or family.

Attributes
Appropriateness, Civility

Kindergarten Skills and Objectives:

Behaving appropriately at social gatherings is an important part of growing up in community with others. In this lesson, children will learn the following:
- To use inside voices when in social gatherings
- To wait nicely in lines
- To exercise civility in other small acts of respect

PART 4

- While at the dinner table, don't talk with your mouth _____.
- If someone has her arms full and is trying to open the door, you should…
- If you accidentally spill something, you should…
- You greet a guest at your party by saying_____.
- When there is a crowd of people you need to get through, you do not shove, but instead say_____.
- If you are at a birthday party and you are invited to play in a game, you should…
- When you leave someone's home, you should say_____.
- If there is a long line, you should…
- When an elderly person is looking for a seat, you should…
- You are serving your plate at a party. How do you put the food on your plate?

> ## Definitions:
>
> **APPROPRIATENESS**
> Knowing the right thing to say or do in any given situation
>
> **CIVILITY**
> To respect others and self for the betterment of community

Lead a discussion with students on why it is important to act respectful when you are with others:

- It makes the experience pleasant for everyone.
- It shows respect for others at the party/gathering.
- It shows that you can be trusted in social settings.
- If you have been invited somewhere, it may lead to a second invitation.

Close the lesson by having children practice Wilbur's civility poem one or two more times.

PART 4

EXTENDING
CHILDREN'S LEARNING

1. Throughout the week, remind students of how to "just act respectful" in different community situations by pulling scenarios out of the JAR and asking students to tell you what the right behavior would be. If time allows, let them act this out for you.

2. Read *Lyle and the Birthday Party* by Bernard Waber (Sandpiper, 1973). At various times, stop and discuss with the children what is happening in the story and how Lyle is feeling. Let them partner-talk as you read, stopping at different points to talk about shyness, maturity, behaving appropriately in social places and complaining.

3. Read *Moria's Birthday* by Robert Munch (Annick Press, 1992) to further discuss appropriate party manners. This is a funny book that will help you illustrate inappropriate behavior. Have the students fix the funny party mistakes as you are reading.

4. Host a Manners Party. Have the students create invitations and decorations with classroom art supplies. Guide the children as they plan a party to show off their newly learned social manners. Assign children jobs (greeter, servers, cleaners, and parting gift presenters) to make the party go smoothly. Practice in your classroom before the party with close teacher observation so that the students will practice the skills correctly. You may want to invite the principal, secretary, enrichment teachers, cafeteria staff, cleaning staff, or parents. Do what works for you in your school. This will take lots of practice and teacher intervention. Serve cookies and juice with plates and napkins. Refer to the lessons on "Being a Host" and "Respecting the Property of Others" to remind students what they have learned about being good hosts and about cleaning up messes.

PART 4

Home Connection

Dear Parent/Guardian,

This week, your kindergartner is beginning to learn about exercising civility in your community by "acting respectfully" in social situations. Here is an activity you can do at home to reinforce what your child is learning at school:

Make a "Just Act Respectful" JAR by cutting out the scenarios below and placing them in a large jar. At the dinner or breakfast table, pull a couple of slips out of the jar and lead a family discussion on the appropriate way to deal with the social situation on the slip of paper. You may also make up your own scenarios for future "Just Act Respectful" discussions on civility.

~ From Our Hearts To Yours

If you see someone drop something, you should… *Help them pick it up!*	If a friend gives you a present and you already have one, you should say… *Thank you! (This looks like fun!)*	If you don't like the food being served, you should… *Still eat a "courtesy bite" or say, "No, thank you" with a smile!*	When an elderly person is looking for a seat, you should… *Offer him/her your seat!*
If you are eating with others and you finish your meal first, you should… *Sit quietly and enjoy the conversation!*	If someone has her arms full and is trying to open the door, you should… *Open the door for her!*	When a guest is leaving, you should say… *Thank you very much for coming! I had fun!*	When you leave someone's home, you should say… *Thank you for having me! I had fun!*
Show me the kind of voice you should use if you are at a gathering with friends or family… *Your inside voice! (No yelling!)*	If you are at a birthday party and you are invited to play in a game, you should… *Play!*	When there is a crowd of people you need to get through, you do not shove, but say… *Please excuse me!*	How do you put food on your plate at a party? *With a serving utensil or touching only the one you are taking!*

Just Act Respectful

If you see someone drop something, you should… *Help them pick it up!*	If a friend gives you a present and you already have one, you should say… *Thank you! (This looks like fun!)*
If you are eating with others and you finish your meal first, you should… *Sit quietly and enjoy the conversation!*	If you don't like the food being served, you should… *Still eat a "courtesy bite" or say, "No, thank you" with a smile!*
When a guest is leaving, you should say… *Thank you very much for coming! I had fun!*	Show me the kind of voice you should use if you are at a gathering with friends or family… *Your inside voice! (No yelling!)*
While at the dinner table, don't talk with your mouth… *Full! (Close your mouth to chew and then you can talk!)*	If someone has her arms full and is trying to open the door, you should… *Open the door for her!*
If you accidentally spill something, you should… *Clean it up!*	You greet a guest at your party by saying… *Hello! Thank you for coming!*
When there is a crowd of people you need to get through, you do not shove, but instead say… *Please excuse me!*	If you are at a birthday party and you are invited to play in a game, you should… *Play!*
When you leave someone's home, you should say… *Thank you for having me! I had fun!*	If there is a long line, you should… *Wait nicely for your turn! (Don't complain!)*
When an elderly person is looking for a seat, you should… *Offer him/her your seat!*	How do you put food on your plate at a party? *With a serving utensil or touching only the one you are taking!*

Chapter 20

Respecting Your Country

On a beautiful Sunday afternoon, the soon-to-be-graduates of a large high school filed onto the floor of a college basketball arena to take their seats for the baccalaureate ceremony. Family members and friends were seated in the balcony overlooking the floor. A ninety-something-year-old gentleman was seated in a wheelchair near the stage for an up-close view of his great-grandson's graduation.

The music of the drum and bugle corps resonated in the massive space as they entered the arena for the playing of the national anthem, but the beating of the drums couldn't drown out the noisy chatter in the crowd. Even the students being honored continued talking as the familiar notes of "O, say can you see…" filled the air. No one was looking for the flag. No one placed a hand over their heart. No one even tried to sing the words.

Except for one man.

The old gentleman maneuvered his chair to face the flag. He leaned down and lifted one foot and then the other from their platforms to the floor. With all the strength he could muster, his withered hands gripped the arms of his chair to enable him to stand erect. His first attempt failed. A second attempt failed. By sheer determination, he finally made it to his feet. By sheer willpower, he lifted his right hand and placed it over his heart. His frail body found strength through the power of his patriotism.

Did the fans at the last high school football game you attended stand with hands over their hearts for the playing of the national anthem? Did they mouth the words, even if they couldn't sing the notes? Did anyone turn toward the flag?

We can bring a return of true patriotism to this generation. We can instill an appreciation for the freedoms that we enjoy in our country. We can help children develop a deep love and respect for all that our country stands for. We can generate a desire to stand and say, "I'm proud to be an American."

In this week's lesson, kindergartners will learn the significance of our flag. We'll help you teach the Pledge of Allegiance to your first graders. The story behind the writing of The national anthem will come alive for second-graders. Finally, third-graders will learn what it means to become a citizen who is a patriot.

As Alexis de Tocqueville said in 1835, "America is great because she is good. If America ceases to be good, America will cease to be great."

We can help this generation ensure America will continue to be great because they will make certain she is good.

PART 4

| **199**

Big Ideas

- When we teach children to appreciate the freedoms of our country, we help them develop respect for those who defend our country.
- The Pledge of Allegiance not only teaches children to respect our flag, but learning the meaning of the words helps them understand the importance of keeping our promises.
- America will forever be great, as long as her people remain good.

Grade-level skills and objectives:

(K) Understanding how and why the American flag was made and what it symbolizes becomes the foundation of developing respect for our country.

(1) Learning the meaning of the Pledge of Allegiance helps children understand that the Pledge is a promise we make to honor our country.

(2) Sharing the story behind our country's national anthem helps children develop a deeper respect for our nation.

(3) Learning appreciation for our soldiers creates a desire to become a good citizen of our country.

PART 4

Stars and Stripes

Materials and Preparation

- Wise Ol' Wilbur puppet
- American flag
- "The Little Patriot with a Big Heart" (found at the end of this lesson)
- (Optional) Patriotic music
- (Optional) Color the "Old Glory" activity sheet ahead of time or find an image of it online (1 total)

To present this lesson, you could use a sewing basket or large basket filled with pieces of red, white and blue fabrics, needles, thread and scissors as a prop.

NOTE: If you want to try your hand at cutting Betsy Ross' five-point star pattern, visit http://www.ushistory.org/betsy/flagstar.html. Your students will be fascinated if you demonstrate the technique for cutting a five-point star with just one snip!! However, don't wait till the last minute; it will take a little practice to fold the paper correctly.

Wilbur's Words of Wisdom

Show respect for the flag;
Don't let it touch the ground.
Show respect for the flag;
Not just when others are around.
Show respect for the flag;
Place your hand on your heart.
Show respect for the flag;
For your country – play your part.

Guiding Children's Learning

(Optional: To engage the students in a fun way from the start, strike up the patriotic music for the beginning of this lesson.) Ask one child to march around the room carrying the flag at attention; if needed, remind your volunteer of this high honor and important responsibility. After the student has made one lap around the room, tell your students that today they're going to learn how to show respect for the flag of our country.

Attributes

Citizenship, Patriotism

Kindergarten Skills and Objectives:

Understanding how and why the American flag was made and what it symbolizes becomes the foundation of developing respect for our country. In this lesson, children will learn the following:

- To respect our flag by never putting it on the floor
- To stand and place your hand over your heart when you see the flag
- To keep your eyes on the flag

PART 4

Using the Wise Ol' Wilbur puppet, give the following instructions while having students act them out, when appropriate:

- Whenever you see the flag, stand and place your right hand over your heart. This is to show your love for your country and for the people who have fought for her.
- Turn and follow the flag as it passes by, keeping your eyes on the flag.
- It is important never to let the flag touch the floor.

Ask another student to march around the room carrying the flag at attention. Encourage your students to place their right hands on their hearts, as they watch the flag pass by.

Ask the children to be seated while you explain the story of our flag, using the following:

- Explain that our first flag was handmade by Betsy Ross at the request of George Washington, our first president.
- Show the "Old Glory" activity sheet of our first flag with thirteen stars. (If time allows, have a sample colored for them ahead of time.)
- Explain that the stars of the first flag represented the first thirteen colonies. (The colonies later became states after the Declaration of Independence was signed.)
- Explain that as we added more and more states, more and more stars were added on our flag until today we have fifty stars for our fifty states (indicate this on the flag). If another state is added to our country, another star will be added to our flag on the fourth of July following the addition of the new state!
- Explain that the stripes also represent the thirteen original states. The top and bottom stripes are red.

Ask the following questions:

- Have any of you ever watched someone sew by hand? (You could make a simple running stitch on a piece of fabric.)
- How many stars do you see on this flag? (Help them count the thirteen stars.)

Now, explain that the colors of our flag are also very important:

- White reminds us to be good and pure.
- Red reminds us to be brave.
- Blue reminds us never to give up.

Definitions:

CITIZENSHIP
An attitude of cooperation and social responsibility

PATRIOTISM
Loving our country enough to protect it and the principles upon which it was

If time allows, read "The Little Patriot with a Big Heart." Afterwards, ask:

- How do Grandpa and Jack show respect for the flag?
    - They never allowed the flag to touch the floor.
    - They stood with hands over their hearts.

PART 4

To close, teach students **Wilbur's Words of Wisdom**. Have Wilbur remind students of the following:

- Respecting our flag shows respect for our country and for the men and women who have fought for our country.
- Whenever you see the flag, stand and place your right hand over your heart.
- Respect our flag by never putting it on the floor.

EXTENDING
CHILDREN'S LEARNING

1. Give each child a copy of the "Our Flag" and "Old Glory" activity sheets. Ask them to color the flags in red, white and blue. Remind them that the first and last stripes are red on both flags! If possible, laminate each flag and post them in your room to display the patriotism of your class.

2. Help your students make their own flag using 6½" x 12" pieces of red construction paper (1/student), ½" x 12" strips of white construction paper (6/student), and 3½" x 5½" rectangles of blue construction paper (1/student). You will also need glue sticks and white chalk for each student.

   Using the red construction paper for the base, students can glue the white strips in place. Then, have them glue the blue construction paper in the top left corner on top of the strips. They can use the chalk to draw stars on the blue rectangle.

3. Set up for Flag Tag Relay! You will need a small flag on a stick for each student. Put sand in two buckets and place them on the ground next to each other. Stick half of the flags into one bucket and stick the other half into the second bucket. Divide the children into two teams and line them up far enough away for a relay. When you say go, let the kids run and pick a flag. Then have them march back to the line and tag the next player. Continue on until all of the flags are out of the bucket and in the hands of the children. When the team is finished, have the students hold their flag HIGH to indicate completion.

4. Celebrate Flag Day everyday in your classroom. Each morning, let one student march around the classroom with the flag while the rest of the class stands at attention, hands over hearts, turning toward the flag as it goes by. Your children will quickly make the habit to show respect any time they see the flag!

5. Invite a veteran or soldier to your class to tell about his or her love for our country and willingness to fight for our country. Ask your guest to share what the American flag means to him/her after serving in our military.

PART 4

| **203**

Home Connection

Dear Parent/Guardian,

Understanding how and why the American flag was made and what it symbolizes becomes the foundation of developing respect for our country. This week, our goal is to help your child develop respect for the American flag and all that it represents. In this lesson, children are learning the following:

- Respecting our flag shows respect for our country.
- We respect our flag by placing a hand over our heart and by never letting it touch the ground.

If you would like to reinforce your child's development of respect for our country, here are a few ideas:

- Ask yourself, are you modeling respect for our country to your child? Did you stand at the last high school football game with your hand over your heart for the national anthem? Did you sing along? Did you turn toward the flag? Did you remove your hat?

- It's very easy to criticize the president, to complain about everything that's wrong with our country and to talk about how disgruntled we are with the state of our society. Instead of complaining, do your best to let your child see you doing something to make our country better, to see you are being the best citizen you can possibly be. He needs to witness your respect and love for 'the land of the free and the home of the brave,' if he is ever going to develop respect for our country himself.

~ From Our Hearts To Yours

Our Flag

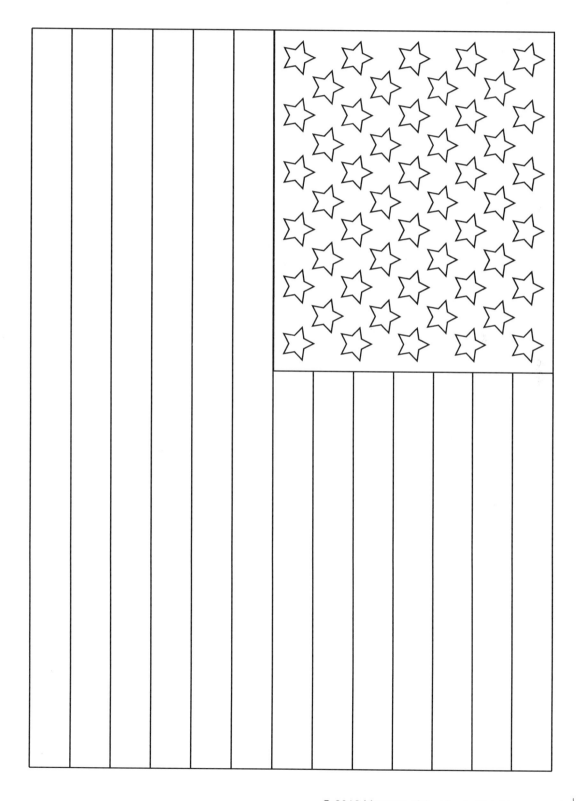

PART 4

Old Glory

|

PART 4

THE LITTLE PATRIOT
WITH A BIG HEART

Jack's grandpa lived in one of those great old houses with a big front porch on Walnut Street in Merryville. Jack loved playing checkers with his grandpa on the big front porch.

When Jack lost a game, Grandpa would always say, "Let's go for two out of three." The day they went for five out of nine, Grandpa decided it was time to take a break from checkers. He patted Jack on the shoulder and said, "Jack, why don't you go look in my bedroom closet for an old brown shoebox that holds my marble collection. I want to show you the champion marble my grandpa gave me when I was your age."

Jack ran to the closet to look for the shoebox, but there were lots of shoeboxes on the floor of Grandpa's closet. The first box he opened was full of letters. He wondered if they were letters from Grandma to Grandpa.

The next box Jack found was full of old fishing baits. He set it aside for later, so he could ask Grandpa about going fishing.

Then Jack saw a brown shoebox taped together sitting in the back corner of the closet. It looked as old as Grandpa. *This has gotta be it,* Jack thought, as he struggled with the tape to get the top off.

When he looked inside, there were no marbles to be found, but brightly colored ribbons and medals with photographs of soldiers. This looked like more fun than marbles, so he picked up the box and ran back to the porch with a hundred questions for Grandpa.

"Grandpa, Grandpa," called Jack. "Look what I found."

"Let's see what ya' got," answered Grandpa with a chuckle.

Jack ran to the table and put the box in front of Grandpa. When Grandpa saw the box, the excitement in his voice turned to sadness.

Seeing the old man's sad face, Jack asked, "What's wrong, Grandpa?"

"Jack, that box is full of old friends. I haven't looked in that box for years and

| **207**

years," said Grandpa.

"Old friends?" questioned Jack. "Are you talking about the pictures of the Army men?"

"Yep, they were my buddies. We fought together in the war," answered Grandpa.

Jack asked, "Will you tell me about 'em?"
Grandpa shook his head from side to side without saying a word.

"Will you pleeeease tell me about 'em, Grandpa?" begged Jack.

"Well, maybe it is time I told you," said Grandpa as he stood and looked at the flag hanging from his porch.

"Grandpa, is this you standing next to the Jeep?" asked Jack holding a picture up so Grandpa could see it.

"That's me, Jack."

"Where were you, Grandpa?"

"I was stationed in a little town in France."

"Where's France, Grandpa?"

"It's a country across the ocean in Europe."

While Grandpa was answering his questions, Jack kept digging in the box. He found an envelope with a rubber band around it that had something hard inside. As he took the rubber band off to open the envelope, Jack said, "You've never told me about the war, Grandpa."

"I don't talk about it much because some of my buddies didn't come home," said Grandpa.

Jack said, "What do you mean, they didn't come home?"

Grandpa was still looking at the flag when he answered, "They died in battle and were buried over there. They gave up their lives fighting for our freedom."

"What's this?" asked Jack as he opened the envelope to find a silver star attached to a ribbon. "This looks important, Grandpa."

Grandpa turned to see what Jack was holding. When he saw the medal in Jack's hand, he asked Jack to put it back as a tear welled up in his eye.

"What is it? Is it yours? Are you a hero?" asked Jack in rapid-fire succession.

The single tear in Grandpa's eye became a flood of tears that rolled down his face.

"I got that for pulling some guys out of danger, but that didn't make me a hero," said Grandpa. "My buddies were the real heroes. They were real patriots."

"What's a patriot, Grandpa?"

"A patriot is someone who loves his country. He does his part to keep America a great nation by being a good citizen," answered Grandpa.

"How can I be a patriot, Grandpa?" asked Jack.

Grandpa's tears slowed as he answered his little grandson's big question. "You can start by showing respect for the 'Stars and Stripes,'" Grandpa said, as he reached out and touched the flag hanging from his porch.

Jack ran over and touched the flag, too. "I've learned a lot about how to take care of the flag at school, Grandpa."

"I'm glad to hear that, Jack," said Grandpa. "I fold this flag every night and hang it out every morning. I never let it touch the floor."

"We learned that rule at school, but I've never met anyone who did it, till you, Grandpa," said Jack with a grin on his face. "I want to learn more about how to be a patriot. Will you teach me?"
"It would be my honor, Jack," said Grandpa, taking great pride in his grandson.

For the next few months, Grandpa made sure Jack learned all the words to "The Star-Spangled Banner." Together, they practiced standing at attention with hands over their hearts at baseball games. Grandpa smiled every time he saw someone in the stands look at his little patriot with his hand over his heart trying to sing the words to our national anthem. Jack smiled every time he saw others put their hands over their hearts.

Jack had been looking forward to the fourth of July this year because of all that Grandpa had taught him about loving his country. He knew the July 4th parade would be the perfect time to use all he had learned.

Jack spent the night with Grandpa the night before the big parade, so they could get a good seat. The parade came right in front of Grandpa's house on Walnut Street.

Sure enough, the next morning crowds came out early with their lawn chairs to line the street. Just as everyone sat down to wait for the parade, they heard the beating of drums, the blowing of horns, and the clashing of cymbals signaling the beginning of the parade.

When Grandpa saw the flag coming, he thought about all the stories he had shared with Jack about his war days. When Jack saw the flag coming, he jumped to his feet, and said, "Grandpa, stand up!"

Grandpa raised his tired old bones out of his chair and stood next to Jack, who was standing proudly with his hand over his heart. As Jack looked down the sidewalk, he saw others begin to stand at attention. All stood except for Sergeant Joe, one of Grandpa's friends, who was sitting in a wheelchair in his Army uniform. He was trying to stand up, but he couldn't quite do it.

Jack knew he needed help, so he ran over to the old gentleman and said, "Lean on me, Sergeant Joe. I'll help you stand." With Jack's help, the Sergeant stood tall and saluted the flag.

Jack's grandpa made his way over to stand with them. He smiled with pride as he stood next to his little patriot with a big heart.

Grandpa dropped his champion marble in Jack's pocket as he patted him on the head.

JUST THE BEGINNING...

PART 4

Chapter 21

Respecting Our Environment

Most of us who grew up in the country long for the simple pleasures of country living. The clean air. The night sky under a blanket of stars and planets. Walks in the woods. The sound of rushing water. Crickets chirping at sundown. Crisp clothes dried on a clothesline.

> **" Our greatest natural resource is the minds of our children.**
>
> -Walt Disney

Country folks understand resourcefulness. Knowing you can't run to the corner market to pick up more paper makes you count every piece of paper as precious. Knowing how hard your uncle works to have a good crop of beans makes you aware of the size of your portions at the dinner table. Knowing how dark it is in the country after sundown makes you appreciate the wonderful invention of electricity.

Most of us who grew up in the country also grew up with little. Truth is, we didn't need much. We understand the truth in the old adage, 'Necessity is the mother of invention.' If you know that what you have won't be replaced, you take better care of what you have. If your family can't afford the latest and greatest, you learn to appreciate what you can afford. If you couldn't have the expensive 'stuff,' you made up your own fun, which was even better because you found a sense of pride in your ingenuity.

Teaching children to take care of our environment means much more than 'green' living. It's helping children understand that less is more exciting, more challenging, more really more — resourceful.

It's helping them develop a conscientious spirit that desires to take care of our surroundings for the good of everyone.

PART 4

Big Ideas

- Teaching children to respect their environment helps to instill an appreciation for what they have.
- Learning to conserve our resources develops the imagination, allowing children to be creative and inventive.
- The old adage, "Necessity is the mother of invention," holds true today.

Grade-level skills and objectives:

(K) Children develop resourcefulness when they are encouraged to conserve.

(1) When children learn that trash belongs in the trash, not in the street, they discover they can make a big difference in keeping their city clean.

(2) Recognizing that trash doesn't disappear when you throw it away, children learn the importance of reusing and recycling.

(3) Children learn they have a part to play in keeping their environment clean so everyone can enjoy the beauty of the surroundings—indoors and outdoors.

PART 4

Waste Not, Want Not

Materials and Preparation

- (Optional) One night light*

*This can be plugged into an extension cord to make it easier for the children to reach.

Wilbur's Words of Wisdom

The *environment* is meant for you and me!

You Can Save

Switch off the lights when you leave.

Turn off the faucet if you please.

You can help ev'ry day.

When you think, You can save!

Guiding Children's Learning

(Optional: Introduce the lesson by showing the children the nightlight. Allow them to take turns turning the switch on and off.) Ask the class, When is a good time to use a night light?
- *At night.*
- *When it's dark.*

When do you not need a night light?
- *During the day*
- *When it's light in the day*

Begin the lesson with a discussion:

Do you remember what you have learned from *Manners of the Heart* in the last few lessons?
- *To respect adults*
- *To respect the team*

Attributes

Conscientiousness, Resourcefulness

Kindergarten Skills and Objectives:

Children develop resourcefulness when they are encouraged to conserve food, electricity, water and paper. In this lesson, children will learn the following:
- To turn off the lights when not in use
- To turn off the faucet when it is not in use
- To flush the toilet only when it needs to be flushed
- To not take more than they can eat or drink

- *To respect differences*
- *To respect the rights and the privacy of others*
- *To respect property*
- *To respect others in my community*
- *To respect our flag and our country*

- That's right! Today, we're going to talk about respecting our environment. Do you know what our environment is?

- Many times, when people talk about the environment, they are talking about natural surroundings in the world. They are talking about the trees, the sky, the ocean and the animals. Look around the room. An environment is any area that surrounds you. This is your classroom environment.

> ## Definitions:
>
> **CONSCIENTIOUSNESS**
> Diligent carefulness
>
> **RESOURCEFULNESS**
> Finding creative solutions to everyday problems; using your imagination and mind to re-purpose materials

- Everyone in the world shares in this environment. Since we all have to share this environment, we need to do our part in always taking care of it.

What are some ways to take care of the environment? (Help them with the following, if needed.)
- *Turn off the radio and television when they are not in use.*
- *Turn off the lights when you are not using them.*
- *Turn off the water after washing hands.*
- *Don't leave the water running when you're brushing your teeth.*
- *Don't leave the refrigerator door open for a long time.*
- *Close the door behind you when you're going and coming at home.*
- *Recycle your soda cans, glass bottles and plastic containers.*
- *Pass the clothes you've outgrown to a brother or sister or to someone who needs them.*

Reinforce the following important ways students can help to take care of our environment:

When you leave the room, remember to…
- *Turn off the lights.*

When you are brushing your teeth, you should…
- *Turn off the water until you need to rinse.*

Flush the toilet only…
- *When it needs flushing; toilets are not for playing.*

When you are serving your plate, you should…

PART 4

- *Take only what you can eat or drink.*

Now, to help your students remember today's lesson, teach them Wilbur's "You Can Save" chant under **"Wilbur's Words of Wisdom."**

Close the lesson with a review of the four important behaviors they can practice to help our environment. Explain that everyone benefits when each person does his or her part.

EXTENDING
CHILDREN'S LEARNING

1. Have children create a beautiful piece of art while practicing resourcefulness. Place old magazines in the art center along with scissors and glue. Have each student find one or more pictures of the environment and help them cut this picture out to make a class collage on poster board. Each student should contribute a picture toward the collage. At the end, explain that each of them had a part in making the collage, just as we all have a part in protecting our environment. Display the environment collage attractively in the classroom and write the following sentence underneath: "Our environment is meant for you and me."

2. To reinforce your students' understanding of resourcefulness and conserving energy, have each student bring recyclables from home (e.g., egg cartons, empty cereal or food boxes, plastic bottles, caps, etc.). Place the trash in the art area where they can make sculptures with glitter, sequins, paper, markers and glue. Explain that "trash" can sometimes be used and does not always need to be thrown away. Display their sculptures in the classroom or school library for others to see or have an art show for parents and other family members.

3. Adopt a flowerbed at school. Have children plant seasonal flowers and tend it as necessary. This will give them a greater appreciation for protecting their environment and wanting to do their part in making it beautiful.

4. Create a classroom policy on conserving the energy in your school. Come up with specific ways students can help. Here are some ideas:

   - Assign a student to turn your lights on or off when you enter and leave the classroom throughout each day.
   - When washing hands, have students remind each other to turn off the faucet when using soap, in between rinsing.
   - As a class, decide on the number of paper towels or napkins students should take each time they wash their hands or eat a snack.
   - Decide on a fun way to correct the student who takes too much food at lunch time and does not finish it. Continue to remind students to take only as much food as they need each day.

Home Connection

Dear Parent/Guardian,

As Wilbur says, "The *environment* is meant for you and me!" This week, children are learning to respect the environment that they share with others. Kindergartners are learning to conserve electricity, water and food in the following ways:

- By turning off lights when not in use
- By turning off the faucet when it is not in use
- By flushing the toilet only when it needs to be flushed
- By not taking more than they can eat or drink

Here are a few ideas for you to reinforce what your child is learning at school:

- Write each of the following statements on a slip of paper and put them in a jar. These are examples of things your child can do to show respect for the environment. Each night, pull one slip from the jar and have your child tell the appropriate way to respond.

    When you leave the room, remember to…
    Turn off the lights.

    When you are brushing your teeth you should….
    Turn off the water until you need to rinse.

    Flush the toilet only…
    When it needs flushing; toilets are not for playing.

    When you are serving your plate, you should…
    Take only what you can eat or drink.

- As a family, choose a service project that encourages resourcefulness rather than wastefulness. For example, participate in a coat or clothes drive for the needy or make holiday gifts out of recycled materials for the elderly in a nursing home.

- Remind your child to limit waste when eating. For example, teach him not to grab unnecessary packs of condiments or napkins that will just get thrown away. Remind your child to take or order only as much food as he can eat or suggest that he split or share a meal with you or a friend.

- Look for opportunities to purchase recycled school supplies like construction paper or pencils. Teach the importance of using recycled materials.

~ From Our Hearts To Yours

Appendix

Common Core State Standards Alignment

Kindergarten Common Core Alignment Chart	Intro	Chapter 1	Chapter 2	Chapter 3	Chapter 4	Chapter 5	Chapter 6	Chapter 7	Chapter 8	Chapter 9	Chapter 10	Chapter 11	Chapter 12	Chapter 13	Chapter 14	Chapter 15	Chapter 16	Chapter 17	Chapter 18	Chapter 19	Chapter 20	Chapter 21
Reading Literature																						
RL.K.1 With prompting and support, ask and answer questions about key details in a text.	•	•	•	•	•	•	•		•					•			•	•			•	
RL.K.3 With prompting and support, identify characters, settings, and major events in a story.	•		•	•	•									•			•					
RL.K.4 Ask and answer questions about unknown words in a text.	•		•	•	•	•	•	•		•				•	•		•				•	
Writing																						
W.K.2 Use a combination of drawing, dictating, and writing to compose informative/explanatory texts in which they name what they are writing about and supply some information about the topic.	•												•					•			•	
Speaking & Listening																						
SL.K.1 Participate in collaborative conversations with diverse partners about kindergarten topics and texts with peers and adults in small and larger groups.	•	•	•	•	•	•	•	•	•	•	•	•	•	•	•	•	•	•	•	•	•	•
SL.K.2 Confirm understanding of a text read aloud or information presented orally or through other media by asking and answering questions about key details and requesting clarification if something is not understood.	•	•	•	•		•		•	•					•	•	•				•	•	
SL.K.3 Ask and answer questions in order to seek help, get information, or clarify something that is not understood.	•	•	•	•	•					•				•		•		•		•	•	•
SL.K.4 Describe familiar people, places, things, and events and, with prompting and support, provide additional detail.			•	•		•	•	•	•					•	•		•	•	•			
SL.K.5 Add drawings or other visual displays to descriptions as desired to provide additional detail.	•				•	•	•	•	•												•	
SL.K.6 Speak audibly and express thoughts, feelings, and ideas clearly.	•	•	•	•	•	•	•	•	•	•	•	•	•	•	•	•	•	•	•	•	•	•
Social Studies																						
K.4.1 Identify individuals in a position of authority within a family, school, or community and their responsibilities.														•	•			•				
K.4.2 Explain the importance of rules at home, class, and school.			•	•			•					•	•		•	•		•	•		•	•
K.4.3 Discuss the roles, rights, and responsibilities of being a good citizen in a family, class, and school.	•	•	•	•	•	•			•					•	•	•	•	•	•	•	•	•

Pre and Post Assessment Instrument

Teacher Survey

Teacher Name: _____ Grade (select one): K 1 2 3 4 5

School Name: _____ Date: _____

	Never					Sometimes					Always
1. My students use good manners.	0	10	20	30	40	50	60	70	80	90	100
2. My students make friends easily.	0	10	20	30	40	50	60	70	80	90	100
3. My students are helpful to me and others.	0	10	20	30	40	50	60	70	80	90	100
4. My students look for others who need help.	0	10	20	30	40	50	60	70	80	90	100
5. My students are patient when they need to wait.	0	10	20	30	40	50	60	70	80	90	100
6. My students help others by being a friend in times of need.	0	10	20	30	40	50	60	70	80	90	100
7. My students say, "I'm sorry," if they make a mistake.	0	10	20	30	40	50	60	70	80	90	100
8. My students congratulate others for a job well done.	0	10	20	30	40	50	60	70	80	90	100
9. My students show others that they care about them.	0	10	20	30	40	50	60	70	80	90	100
10. My students stop (and listen) when someone is talking to them.	0	10	20	30	40	50	60	70	80	90	100
11. My students look someone in the eye when they are speaking.	0	10	20	30	40	50	60	70	80	90	100
12. My students listen to what other people are saying.	0	10	20	30	40	50	60	70	80	90	100
13. My students are patient with each other.	0	10	20	30	40	50	60	70	80	90	100
14. My students give words of encouragement to others who fail.	0	10	20	30	40	50	60	70	80	90	100
15. My students treat others the way they want to be treated.	0	10	20	30	40	50	60	70	80	90	100
16. My students act like it is better to give than receive.	0	10	20	30	40	50	60	70	80	90	100
17. My students are generous with each other.	0	10	20	30	40	50	60	70	80	90	100
18. My students use their inside voices inside.	0	10	20	30	40	50	60	70	80	90	100
19. My students appreciate the efforts of others.	0	10	20	30	40	50	60	70	80	90	100
20. My students try to be ladies and gentlemen.	0	10	20	30	40	50	60	70	80	90	100
21. My boy students allow girls and elders to go first.	0	10	20	30	40	50	60	70	80	90	100
22. My girl students thank boys who act like gentlemen.	0	10	20	30	40	50	60	70	80	90	100
23. My students are good hosts when given the opportunity.	0	10	20	30	40	50	60	70	80	90	100
24. My students are polite guests.	0	10	20	30	40	50	60	70	80	90	100
25. My students respect me.	0	10	20	30	40	50	60	70	80	90	100
26. My students are caring.	0	10	20	30	40	50	60	70	80	90	100
27. My students are honest.	0	10	20	30	40	50	60	70	80	90	100
28. My students are respectful.	0	10	20	30	40	50	60	70	80	90	100
29. My students are responsible.	0	10	20	30	40	50	60	70	80	90	100
30. My students greet adults with a smile and/or a warm greeting.	0	10	20	30	40	50	60	70	80	90	100
31. My students greet adults with a handshake.	0	10	20	30	40	50	60	70	80	90	100
32. My students listen when someone else is talking.	0	10	20	30	40	50	60	70	80	90	100
33. My students speak without interrupting someone else's turn.	0	10	20	30	40	50	60	70	80	90	100
34. My students speak politely to adults.	0	10	20	30	40	50	60	70	80	90	100
35. My students show respect when adults are speaking to them.	0	10	20	30	40	50	60	70	80	90	100
36. My students look for ways to encourage others.	0	10	20	30	40	50	60	70	80	90	100
37. My students perform thoughtful acts.	0	10	20	30	40	50	60	70	80	90	100

Activities and Attributes Chart

Week	Lesson Title	Attributes	Story	Craft	Game	Activity Sheet	Discussion	Instruction on Board	Poster or Cards	Role Play	Song/Cheer Poem	Group Brainstorm	Props	Puppets	Technology: Flipcharts
	Introductory Lesson Manners in Merryville	Manners in the Heart	•			•	•							•	
Part 1: Manners of the Heart															
1	**Helping Others** Helping at Home	Kindness Love	•			•	•				•		•		•
2	**Excusing Others and Excusing Me** Wait, Wait, Wait	Humility Patience	•				•				•			•	
3	**Appreciating Others** Applauding Others	Appreciation Encouragement	•		•	•					•				
4	**Respecting Others** Stop, Look and Listen	Goodness Respectfulness	•				•				•				•
5	**Treating Others** Golden Lessons	Empathy Humility Selflessness	•				•								
Part 2: Everyday Courtesies															
6	**Becoming Ladies and Gentlemen** You Go First	Gentleness Graciousness	•				•				•				
7	**Being a Host** Thank You For Coming!	Generosity Hospitality					•				•	•	•		
8	**Being a Guest** You Say Hello and I Say Good-bye	Appreciation Politeness	•				•			•	•	•			
Part 3: Communication Skills															
9	**Greetings and Introductions** Friends-to-Be	Friendliness Maturity					•				•				
10	**Conversations** Do You Hear What I Hear?	Participation Self-Control			•		•				•				
11	**Telephone Manners** "Hello, Harris Residence."	Consideration Politeness					•			•	•	•			
12	**Written Communication** A Picture is Worth a Thousand Words	Expressiveness Thoughtfulness			•		•								
Part 4: Living in Community															
13	**Respecting Adults** Yes, Sir - Yes, Ma'am	Honor Obedience	•	•			•				•			•	
14	**Respecting the Team** Your Turn First	Cooperation Selflessness Sportsmanship			•	•	•				•		•	•	
15	**Respecting Differences** You're Different, Just Like Me	Acceptance Understanding			•		•			•					
16	**Respecting Others' Rights** What's Mine is Yours	Empathy Kindness	•				•				•				•
17	**Respecting Others' Privacy** Don't Burst Their Bubbles	Consideration Trustworthiness	•				•				•				
18	**Respecting Property** If You Spill it... Clean it Up!	Appreciation Responsibility	•								•		•	•	
19	**Respecting Your Community** Social Graces for Social Places	Appropriateness Civility				•	•				•	•	•		•
20	**Respecting Your Country** Stars and Stripes	Citizenship Patriotism	•	•	•						•	•	•	•	•
21	**Respecting Our Environment** Waste Not, Want Not	Conscientiousness Resourcefulness									•	•			

| **219**

Materials Chart

Ch.	Lesson Title	Materials Needed
	Introductory Lesson Manners in Merryville	• "Welcome to Merryville" (found at the end of the lesson) • Wise Ol' Wilbur, Peter and Penelope puppets • Copies of Map of Merryville (1/student) • Coloring utensils
Part 1: Attitudes of the Heart		
1	**Helping Others** Helping at Home	Optional Items: • Copies of "Here We Go 'Round the Happle Tree" (1 for you or 1/student) • Laundry basket • Assorted pieces of clothing and/or towels • A few toys from your learning center *(Optional) Your students' shoes
2	**Excusing Others and Excusing Me** Wait, Wait, Wait	• "The Tortoise and the Skunk" (found at the end of the lesson) • Wise Ol' Wilbur puppet
3	**Appreciating Others** Applauding Others	• Copy of the "CHEER" sign (1 total) • Copy of the "TRY AGAIN" sign (1 total) • (Optional) Print each sign on cardstock and glue or tape each to a craft stick
4	**Respecting Others** Stop, Look and Listen	• Practice singing "Stop, Look and Listen," so you can teach your students.
5	**Treating Others** Golden Lessons	• "Albert and the Happle Tree" (found at the end of the lesson)
Part 2: Everyday Courtesies		
6	**Becoming Ladies and Gentlemen** You Go First	• None
7	**Being a Host** Thank You For Coming	• Peter puppet • "Peter is Hosting" script
8	**Being a Guest** You Say Hello and I Say Goodbye!	• Peter puppet • "Peter the Polite Guest" Script
Part 3: Communication Skills		
9	**Greetings and Introductions** Friends-to-Be	• Practice the "Hello and Good-bye song" to the tune of "Goodnight, Ladies."
10	**Conversations** Do You Hear What I Hear?	• None
11	**Telephone Manners** "Hello, Harris Residence."	• Styrofoam or plastic cups (2 or more) • 24" string (1 or more) • Tape
12	**Written Communication** A Picture is Worth a Thousand Words	• Plain, white paper (1/student) • Crayons, markers or paint supplies • (Optional) A picture that a child (outside of class) drew for you

Materials Chart

Ch.	Lesson Title	Materials Needed
Part 4: Living in Community		
13	**Respecting Adults** Yes, Sir - Yes, Ma'am	• "I Don't Understand" (found at the end of the lesson) • Wise Ol' Wilbur puppet • (Optional) Recording of "Respect" by Aretha Franklin (Can be found at www.youtube.com) • (Optional) Classroom board with writing utensils
14	**Respecting the Team** Your Turn First	• Peter and Penelope puppets
15	**Respecting Differences** You're Different, Just Like Me	• None
16	**Respecting Others' Rights** What's Mine is Yours	• "The Little Red Hen" (found at the end of the lesson)
17	**Respecting Others' Privacy** Don't Burst Their Bubbles	• Bubbles • Hula-hoop (more than one would be most helpful)
18	**Respecting Property** If You Spill it... Clean it Up!	• Cup of water (1 total) • Crackers (2-3 total) • Paper towels • Small sweeper and dust pan
19	**Respecting Your Community** Social Graces for Social Places	• Large jar • "Just Act Respectful!" activity sheet—with the different scenarios cut and placed in jar
20	**Respecting Your Country** Stars and Stripes	• Wise Ol' Wilbur puppet • American flag • "The Little Patriot with a Big Heart" (found at the end of the lesson) • (Optional) Patriotic music • "Old Glory" activity sheet (colored beforehand or find an image online)
21	**Respecting Our Environment** Waste Not, Want Not	• (Optional) One night light

Extended Learning Academic Alignment

Chapter	Writing and Vocabulary	Reading Comprehension	Critical Thinking and Problem Solving	Listening	Public Speaking	Concentration and Memorization	Self-Regulation and Responsibility	Creativity	Collaboration and Communication
Intro				1	1		5	1, 2, 3, 4	1, 5
1		2, 3	2	2, 3			1, 4	5	1, 5
2		3		3			1, 2, 4		2, 4
3		2	3	1, 2			4		1, 3, 4
4		1	1	1			2, 3, 4	2	2, 3, 4
5			4	1		1	3	2	3, 4
6		5	2, 3	3, 5	3, 4		1, 2, 4	1	2, 3, 4
7	4				5		2, 5	1, 2	1, 2, 3, 4, 5
8		2	2	2, 4		4	1	3	1, 2, 3
9	3			3	1	3	1, 4		2, 4
10				1, 2, 3, 4	3	1, 2, 4	1, 3		1, 2, 3, 4
11				1, 3		3	1, 2, 4	2	1, 2, 4
12	2	1	1	1				2, 3, 4	1, 2, 3, 4
13		3	3	2, 3, 4	2	1	1, 2, 4		1, 2, 3, 4
14		4	4	4	3	3	1, 2		1, 2, 3, 4
15		2, 4	2, 3, 4	2, 3, 4			3	1	1, 2, 4
16		4	2, 3, 4	1, 4	1		2, 3	3, 4	1, 2, 3, 4
17	2	3, 5	3, 5	3, 5			1, 2, 4	2	1, 4
18		5	5	5		4	1, 2, 3, 4	1	1, 3
19		2, 3	1, 2, 3	2, 3			1, 4	4	1, 2, 4
20				5			4	1, 2	3, 5
21			4				1, 2, 3, 4	1, 2, 4	1, 2, 3, 4

Extended Learning Academic Alignment

Chapter	Language Arts	Social Studies	Science	Health/Physical Ed.	Art	Music
Intro	1, 5				2, 3, 4	
1	2, 3			1	5	
2	3		1	2		
3	2, 4	3				1
4	1				2	
5	4				2	1
6	5	2, 3, 4			1	
7	4	3, 5			1	
8	2	1			3	4
9	3	1, 2, 3			4	
10	1, 3			2		
11	1				2	3
12	1, 2	2, 3, 4			2, 3, 4	
13	1, 2, 3, 4					
14	4			1, 2, 3		
15	2, 4	1		3		
16	1, 4	2		3	4	
17	3, 5	4		1	2	
18	5	1				3, 4
19	2, 3	1, 4				
20		1, 2, 3, 4, 5		3	1, 2	
21	4	1, 2, 4	3		1, 2	

Wilbur's Glossary

A

ACCEPTANCE
Treating everyone you meet with the same respect, regardless of differences

APPRECIATION
Recognizing and acknowledging value in people, places and things

APPROPRIATENESS
Knowing the right thing to say or do in any given situation

C

CITIZENSHIP
An attitude of cooperation and social responsibility

CIVILITY
To respect others and self for the betterment of community

CONSCIENTIOUSNESS
Diligent carefulness

CONSIDERATION
Taking into account the feelings of others before you speak or act

COOPERATION
Working with others for everyone's best; choosing to be helpful, not hurtful

E

EMPATHY
Walking in another person's shoes

ENCOURAGEMENT
Offering words to others to build their confidence

EXPRESSIVENESS
Revealing the content of your heart

F

FRIENDLINESS
Welcoming others by offering a quick smile and a kind word

G

GENEROSITY
Gladly and willingly giving your time, your talent and your treasure

GENTLENESS
Speaking and acting with tenderness

GOODNESS
Being kind, compassionate, and forgiving

GRACIOUSNESS
Being courteous, understanding and generous in all situations

|

Wilbur's Glossary

H

HONOR
Valuing the worth of another by showing respect

HOSPITALITY
Serving others with the purpose of making them feel cared for and comfortable

HUMBLE CONFIDENCE
The courage to be your best so that you can help others become their best

HUMILITY
Not caring who gets credit

K

KINDNESS
Showing care and consideration in an unexpected and exceptional way

L

LOVE
Genuinely caring for another, unconditionally

LOYALTY
Faithful devotion

M

MANNERS
Treating others the way you want to be treated

MATURITY
The ability to make the right choice in spite of negative influences

O

OBEDIENCE
Choosing to submit to authority

P

PARTICIPATION
Choosing to be fully involved in the task or project at hand

PATIENCE
Even-tempered endurance

PATRIOTISM
Loving our country enough to protect it and the principles upon which it was founded

POLITENESS
Using kind words and actions in all situations

R

RESOURCEFULNESS
Finding creative solutions to everyday problems; using your imagination and mind to re-purpose materials

RESPECTFULNESS
Treating others with dignity

RESPONSIBILITY

Wilbur's Glossary

Following through on your duties without supervision

S

SELF-CONTROL
The ability to manage yourself when no one is looking

SELF-ESTEEM
Self-absorption presenting itself as self-conceit on one extreme and self-consciousness on the other

SELF-RESPECT
A character trait which comes from treating others with dignity

SELFLESSNESS
Choosing to give of yourself with no expectation of return or consideration of loss

SPORTSMANSHIP
Being more concerned with supporting your team than helping yourself

T

THOUGHTFULNESS
Looking for ways to make others feel loved

TRUSTWORTHINESS
Doing what you say you're going to do when you say you will do it

U

UNDERSTANDING
Looking at others and listening to others without judgment

MANNERS *of the* **HEART**®

Manners of the Heart® is a non-profit organization working to create a more positive moral culture and bring back respect, responsibility and civility to our society. At Manners of the Heart®, we are dedicated to transforming homes, schools and communities through instructional programs designed to build character, strengthen morals, and increase respectfulness among children and adults. This character education, referred to as "Heart Education," is the training of the next generation to have not only head knowledge to lead, but heart knowledge to lead in the right direction.

MANNERS *of the* **HEART**®
215 Royal Street
Baton Rouge, Louisiana 70802
(225) 383-3235
www.mannersoftheheart.org

www.mannersoftheheart.org

Without respect...
teachers cannot teach.

Looking for professional development that leads to transformation? Our presentations offer practical, research-based practices that will enhance teaching skills and increase students' overall achievement. Teachers leave our presentations "motivated to teach with a deeper commitment to excellence." Manners of the Heart® certified trainers motivate their listeners to action. Contact Manners of the Heart® to book one of our skilled trainers to meet your professional development needs.

Our most popular training topics include:
- The Respectful Classroom
- The Trouble with Incentives
- Motivating Students: What Really Works
- Unlocking the Heart of a Bully

www.mannersoftheheart.org

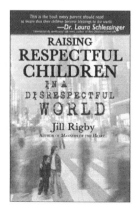
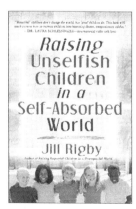

215 Royal Street | Baton Rouge, Louisiana 70802
Phone: 225.383.3235 | www.mannersoftheheart.org

Made in the USA
Lexington, KY
19 August 2015